D0120013

ALL PUNS BLAZING

ALL PUNS BLAZING

THE BEST BRITISH KNOCKOUT JOKES

GEOFF ROWE

and Friends of Leicester Comedy Festival

EBURY
PRESS

3 5 7 9 10 8 6 4 2

Ebury Press, an imprint of Ebury Publishing
20 Vauxhall Bridge Road
London SW1V 2SA

Ebury Press is part of the Penguin Random House group of companies whose
addresses can be found at global.penguinrandomhouse.com

Penguin
Random House
UK

First published by Ebury Press in 2021

www.penguin.co.uk

A CIP catalogue record for this book is available from the British Library

ISBN: 9781529109313

Printed and bound in Great Britain by Clays Ltd, Elcograf S.p.A.
Imported into the EEA by Penguin Random House Ireland,
Morrison Chambers, 32 Nassau Street, Dublin D02 YH68

MIX
Paper from
responsible sources
FSC
www.fsc.org   FSC® C018179

Penguin Random House is committed to a
sustainable future for our business, our readers
and our planet. This book is made from Forest
Stewardship Council® certified paper.

CONTENTS

FOREWORD

Writing 750 words on the history of wordplay is a punishing task. I could start with a whistle-stop tour of punning history, from the ancient Greek playwright Aristophanes to present day computers that generate or evaluate puns. But that wouldn't tell us a lot about what puns are nor how they work.

What even is a pun? Arthur Koestler came up with a precise (if unfunny) definition:

> The pun is the bisociation of a single phonetic form with two meanings – two strings of thought tied together by an acoustic knot. Its immense popularity with children, its prevalence in certain forms of mental disorder ('punning mania'), and its frequent occurrence in the dream, indicate the profound unconscious appeal of association based on pure sound.

Puns play on homonyms (the same word with different meanings) or homophones (different words that sound the same), usually in the hope of raising a laugh. Because languages contain words and sounds that carry more than one meaning, puns are always there, waiting to be discovered.

Today, the pun has something of a bad reputation, and if you groaned at my opening sentence, you just proved my point. However, in Elizabethan England, punning and wordplay were highly prized, and audiences' ears were highly attuned to spotting double meanings. In Shakespeare's plays, even the humble ladies-in-waiting engage in punning battles with their social superiors – presumably with no holds Bard. Ironically, the word 'pun' wasn't even coined till 28 years after Shakespeare died.

The pun's reputation took a dive in the early eighteenth century, in the face of anti-pun polemics by writers like John Dennis and Joseph Addison. By the end of the nineteenth century, George Santayana was calling the pun 'crude and obvious', and in 1905, Sigmund Freud argued that puns were 'the lowest form of verbal joke' because they 'can be made with the least trouble.' Just 20 years ago, pioneering alternative comedian Tony Allen declared himself 'a pun snob', arguing that puns are 'the joke form of the intellectually arrested, of those who are still struggling to understand the basics of language.'

Seen from a different angle, the roots of punning in the acquisition of language might also be the source of its appeal. Freud argued that while very young children are free to enjoy playing with words and sounds as they learn to speak, formal education forces us to stick to strict rules of language. Punning allows us to return to the childhood pleasure of wordplay even in adulthood, and thus he described it as 'liberated nonsense'.

So, puns are pleasurable but reviled. This poses an interesting challenge for the punning comedian – to get past the knee-jerk groans that audiences tend to emit when faced with a pun and allow them to simply enjoy it. With Bec Hill, it's the arts-and-crafty novelty of the way she presents her visual puns. Standing next to a drawing of a teddy bear in sunglasses, she waggles its gun-toting fabric arms in time to the music, before pulling down a paper flap with the words, 'THE RIGHT TO BEAR ARMS' written on it.

With Tim Vine, it's his persona that does it, his sheer silliness. What makes him funny is his slightly desperate delight in his own gags and the way he constantly cajoles and implores the crowd to laugh, not just with what he says ('Come on!'), but also with his widened eyes, grinning mouth and the way he struts around the stage. As soon as he's onstage, he emits a relentless stream of puns, getting a laugh by warning the audience, 'I'm on for three hours.' Another aspect of Vine's appeal is the sheer volume of his punnery. The cover of *Tim Vine Live* boasts that it contains 'AN INCREDIBLE 377 JOKES ON ONE DVD!'.

Similarly, Jimmy Carr turns punning into a feat. After telling the audience he's been trying to write 'the shortest joke possible', he informs them he's written 'a proper joke' that's just four words long: 'Venison's deer isn't it?' Then he ups the ante with a three-word joke: 'Stationery store moves.' Finally, he hits them with an ultra-compact two-worder: 'Dwarf shortage'. Arguably, the framing of these three comedy miniatures is as much a part of the joke as the words themselves. Without the escalating boasts and the way Carr counts each word off on his fingers as he says it, I doubt they'd get the same volume of laughter and applause.

This, then, is the genius of The UK Pun Championships. Framing the act of punning as a sporting contest allows the audience to bypass their cultural aversion and enjoy hearing people playing with words for its own sake. But that's no guarantee that there won't be the odd groan.

Dr Oliver Double (2021)
Head of Comedy and Popular Performance,
University of Kent

A SHORT INTRODUCTION TO LEICESTER COMEDY FESTIVAL AND THE UK PUN CHAMPIONSHIPS

Like many of the very best ideas, the concept for the annual UK Pun Championships was thought up in a pub.

Since 1994, Leicester Comedy Festival (the idea for which was also thought up in a bar) has been proud to celebrate British comedy. Each year, hundreds of comedians gather in the city for the festival to perform over 900 shows across 100 venues.

Over the years the Festival team have developed various concepts for shows, most of which have worked brilliantly. Ideas like 'Comedy in the Dark', a comedy show that takes place (you guessed it) in the dark; 'Hôtel de Comédie', a comedy show that takes place in a hotel, and 'Comedy in a Car' all went down wonderfully.*

---

* Editor's note: I think everyone gets the idea, Geoff!

On the other hand, there was 'Euroversity Challenge' – envisaged as a mash-up of the Eurovision Song Contest and University Challenge … enough said. But I digress because most of the ideas we come up with seem to work or, at least, people enter into the festival spirit and go along with the general idea.

When we started planning for the 2014 Leicester Comedy Festival, we wanted to produce a new show that would be quintessentially British. So, we asked ourselves, what are the most British things about comedy? We pretty quickly came up with … puns! (In fact, it turns out that Australians are pretty keen on puns too, but whatever.)

We had soon dreamt up the notion of The UK Pun Championships, a live battle to find the nation's very best pun comedian every year.

I'd like to give a nod to the many other individuals and teams who were celebrating puns long before us. Promoters like Bec Hill and her 'Pun Run' were really popular, not to mention performers such as Milton Jones, Gary Delaney, Tim Vine and Stewart Francis. There are certainly people who can document the history of puns much better than me; I'm sure there are even PhD studies on the subject, but I'll let you look those up yourself.

There had never been a national celebration of puns before, so we decided to set one up. *Chortle* described one of our first shows as having a 'pantomime atmosphere'. That was deliberate. Yes, there is an overall winner at the event, but we wanted the night to be silly. As silly as puns very often are.

We knew the production of the show was important and had a lot of fun dreaming it all up. Contestants are called 'pun-dits' and walk up to the 'barrel of laughs' to tell their puns (among the physical beer barrels placed onstage), and these days the whole thing is performed in a boxing ring. Part of the inspiration for the show was a boxing match/rap battle, but in the early days we didn't have the right venue to physically host it in a boxing ring.

For the first few years the show took place in Hansom Hall (with the help of our friends at Just the Tonic Comedy Club), but after a few sell-out performances we moved to the much larger De Montfort Hall, where we were able to host the competition in a boxing ring. These days there are sound effects, pyrotechnics and pumping music, plus audience members running around the ring with enormous cards reminding everyone which round we are on. At this point I should give a shout-out to our young American friend, Ben, who attends each year and has become a vital part of the show.

You'll have to come along next year to fully understand what his role involves …

So how does the night work? Each year, it coincides with Twitter's #UKPunDay, where it's best to avoid social media if you aren't a fan of puns. We established this a few years ago and it is now an annual trending Twitter sensation, with thousands of people tweeting their favourite puns, as well as major brands and organisations joining in. It's very silly and we love it.

People enter the show from all over the UK and eight contestants are selected to take part each year. On the night, our brilliant host, comedian Jason Byrne, selects a random topic from the hat (in reality it's a bucket, but you get the idea) and the first pair of pun-dits have to start telling puns based around the selected topic. Some puns are met with wild applause and cheers; others with near silence as the audience tries to figure them out. Sometimes the silence goes on for a while and, just occasionally, there is no laughter at the end of it. But as with the jokes our dads tell, or those we find in our Christmas crackers, the silence and groans are all part of the fun, right?

The eight contestants are eventually whittled down to four, then to two. How are they selected? By the volume of audience whoops and cheers after each round. We've had some amazing pun-dit contestants over the years, and some very worthy winners. I'm hugely grateful to all those who enter, and those who have entered the ring to compete in our ridiculous competition. We are also thankful to the many audience members who come each year for a night of foolishness and to the thousands who take part in #UKPunDay online.

I'm very conscious that there are no puns in this intro; I thought I'd leave that to the wonderful comedians who have generously donated their jokes to help make this book what it is. On which note, special thanks are also due to Fern Beard, who has played an integral part in pulling this book together. And of course, thank you very much for buying it and thank you for supporting

Leicester Comedy Festival, produced by registered charity Big Difference Company.

All the jokes in this collection have been donated and the proceeds will support us going forward so that we can continue to celebrate British comedy and support the emerging talent of the future.

Enjoy!

Geoff Rowe (2021)
Founding Director, Leicester Comedy Festival

HOBBIES

GARDENING

My time as a horticultural rebel was short-lived.
I fought the lawn and the lawn won.

ADELE CLIFF

....

This morning I discovered two deep holes in my
garden with water in them. I thought, 'Well, well'.

RICHARD PULSFORD

....

What new flower grew when my friend
planted a phallic sex toy? A daffodildo.

RICHARD WOOLFORD

....

Michael J. Fox loved gardening but was
overly obsessed with one plant in particular.
He was always going back to the fuchsia.

PHILIP SIMON

....

My gardener is a drag queen and keeps leaving
all her muddy seed packets on the kitchen side.
I'm tired of telling her, 'Sachet, away.'

KAT MOLINARI

....

Without a doubt the rudest gardener
I've ever met was Alan Bitchmarsh.

ADELE CLIFF

....

Someone has clipped my hedges into the
shapes C, A and B. It's topiary out of order.

RICHARD PULSFORD

....

I like my garden ornaments arranged
in gnome particular order.

KAT MOLINARI

....

I dug up my garden and found loads of car parts.
It was a bumper crop. There were more
things buried, but no spoilers!

PHILIP SIMON

....

What's the name of that TV gardener
who's covered in tiny fluffy white sweets?
Alan Titchmarshmallows.

COLIN LEGGO

....

Chris, the passive-aggressive gardener
next door, kept having little digs.

CHRIS NORTON WALKER

....

I'm selling a gardening themed PlayStation game: *Red Shed Redemption*.

CHRIS NORTON WALKER

. . . .

To be an excellent author of gardening books, you need good weeding and writing skills.

STEVIE VEGAS

. . . .

'Mr Fox stole all the farmer's tomatoes,' claimed a mole close to the source.

JOSEPH MURPHY

. . . .

Lion-O, Cheetara and Snarf have been helping me dig up my flower beds. ThunderCats hoe!

COLIN LEGGO

. . . .

Noel Gallagher was asked why he always referred to his younger brother as a flower. He said, 'What, you mean orchid?'

IAIN MACDONALD

. . . .

In order to keep communications going during lockdown, I have been holed up in my garden while talking to my very chatty neighbours. Sometimes it is hard to get a word in hedgeways.

STEVIE VEGAS

. . . .

I was in my garden and noticed some caterpillar
tracks when I was run over by a tank.

JOSEPH MURPHY

....

I was a gardener for many years, but I have since
moved on. It was time to throw in the trowel.

ANDREW TYMMS

....

I like to change the colour of fast-growing
herbs in the garden. Sorry, I dye cress.

IAIN MACDONALD

....

My dad's got a wind farm in his back garden.
I was blown away.

LOVDEV BARPAGA

....

Went to my allotment and found that there
was twice as much soil as there had been
the week before. The plot thickens.

DARREN WALSH

....

This morning I went to the garden centre,
I just spent a couple of hours standing
in the middle of my garden.

TONY COWARDS

....

What's the best thing about being a clumsy florist?
There is no stigma attached.

MASAI GRAHAM

....

I'm going to an ancient garden full of little bearded
men with pointy hats. Well, when in gnome...

LOVDEV BARPAGA

....

What do you call a fake alien garden ornament?
An E.T. faux gnome.

MASAI GRAHAM

....

For Christmas, my wife bought me a book called
How to Build a Swimming Pool in Your Garden.
I'm only a few pages in but I'm digging it!

SEAN HEGARTY

....

I once saw two adjoining gardens try and kiss but
we all know they need tulips for that.

GRAHAM MUSK

....

I came home from work one day and my wife was
watering loads of bottle tops that she'd planted in the
ground. I asked her what she was doing, she said,
'I'm trying to grow a beer garden!'

SEAN HEGARTY

....

Slipped and fell into a purple shrub.
I'll have to be more careful in fuchsia.

DARREN WALSH

....

I've wasted my whole morning watering my
entire garden with a watering can all because
someone said I'm not allowed to use my hose.
Turns out it was a hoax pipe ban.

GRAHAM MUSK

....

I tried growing lots of different flowers over the years,
but in the end I went back to the fuchsias.

KEVIN HUDSON

....

My dog just laid our patio. He's a slabrador.

KEVIN HUDSON

....

'Now, my dears,' said Father Christmas to the three
children, 'here is a present for each of you:
hoe ... hoe ... hoe.'

HENRY DAWE

....

I was in B&Q yesterday when the manager accused
me of shoplifting. Well, I took offence.

NIGEL LOVELL

....

It is hard to grow raisins in the currant climate.

PAUL SAVAGE

....

This tin of fence paint says it requires three coats to apply it properly, and now I'm roasting.

PAUL SAVAGE

....

My baby boy had a flower instead of a head. People ask 'How can you love him?' 'Well, he's still orchid.'

NIGEL LOVELL

....

I turned up at a blind date covered in condensed milk. Apparently, that's not what she meant when she told me to wear Carnation.

NIGEL LOVELL

....

I guess my ultimate dream is to get a breeding pair of lawnmowers, but I'm starting off with something similar, like ladders. Baby steps.

SEAN PATRICK

....

I've become obsessed with landscaping. It started with building a fence, but that was just a gateway to other projects.

PAULINE EYRE

....

I once saw a man lying on his front,
completely naked. Buttock up.

NIGEL LOVELL

. . . .

'What a business last weekend when my son's
friends took over all the rooms in the house.
The only bed that I could find to lie down on was
in the garden: a bed of hardy perennials.'

'Blimey, that can't have been very comfortable.'

'It certainly wasn't. Have you ever
tried resting on your hardies?'

'No, I've only ever rested on my laurels.'

HENRY DAWE

. . . .

My cat is always digging things up in the garden.
I'm going to have her spade.

PAULINE EYRE

. . . .

My mate Geoff is completely lovely, but if you show
him a blue flower he flies into a terrible rage.
He's got a violet temper.

NIGEL LOVELL

. . . .

BOXING

Boxing: what's that, a bout?

RICHARD PULSFORD

· · · · · · · · · · · · · · · · · · · ·

When he was younger, my friend was hit with an
uppercut that made him cry. That's circumcision for you.

ADELE CLIFF

· · · · · · · · · · · · · · · · · · · ·

My boxing opponent hits below the belt and mixes
horrible drinks. He makes some foul punches.

RICHARD PULSFORD

· · · · · · · · · · · · · · · · · · · ·

I'm starting a football team for boxers.
My current star player is Evander Goaliefield.

ADELE CLIFF

· · · · · · · · · · · · · · · · · · · ·

I hear Rocky has hairy palms, must be from
all the times he beat his meat.

RICHARD WOOLFORD

· · · · · · · · · · · · · · · · · · · ·

You'd think I'd be good at boxing considering
I'm bisexual – I'm great at swinging both ways.

KAT MOLINARI

· · · · · · · · · · · · · · · · · · · ·

The prince in *Beauty and the Beast* was a terrible boxer.
Thankfully he was saved by the Belle.

PHILIP SIMON

....

My friend is both a lover and a fighter. I've seen him
deliver a knockout blow; he also does amateur boxing.

ADELE CLIFF

....

The dude from *Rocky* is a stakeholder in many
companies now. Investor Stallone.

KAT MOLINARI

....

Oral fisting. Or as boxers call it: sucker punch.

PHILIP SIMON

....

Which boxer is best at card games? Frank Uno

CHRIS NORTON WALKER

....

Muhammad Ali and George Foreman once had a
famous boxing match at a second-hand clothes
sale: the Rumble in the Jumble.

COLIN LEGGO

....

Did you hear Mike Tyson blew Dracula?
He went down for the Count.

JOSEPH MURPHY

....

I have just been given the go-ahead to award gold, silver and bronze to boxers who cheat on their wives. I really don't think I should be meddling in these affairs.

STEVIE VEGAS

· · · · · · · · · · · · · · · · · · · ·

I didn't like boxing till I first got hit. After that, I was hooked.

PAULINE EYRE

· · · · · · · · · · · · · · · · · · · ·

Back in the eighties and nineties, lots of boxers who turned up to fight were really creased. Apparently, they often had to iron Mike Tyson.

COLIN LEGGO

· · · · · · · · · · · · · · · · · · · ·

Would do more computer boxing puns but I've been saved by the Dell.

CHRIS NORTON WALKER

· · · · · · · · · · · · · · · · · · · ·

I'm launching a boxing-themed curry restaurant at the top of a mountain. It's called the Thai of the Eiger.

ROB THOMAS

· · · · · · · · · · · · · · · · · · · ·

I keep pictures of all my fights from outside the ring in my scrapbook.

STEVIE VEGAS

· · · · · · · · · · · · · · · · · · · ·

Float like a clock, sting like a bee.
That's why they call me Muhammad Dalí.

JOSEPH MURPHY

. . . .

How do you defeat a featherweight champion?
With a knockout blow.

ANDREW TYMMS

. . . .

What did the referee say to the fat boxer to let
him know more food had just arrived?
'Seconds out, round one.'

IAIN MACDONALD

. . . .

Did you see the boxer who got really cross when
his vacuum cleaner broke? Dyson Fury.

KEVIN HUDSON

. . . .

I've written a song about a boxing tournament.
So let me kick off with one of the first versus.

GRAHAM MUSK

. . . .

I bought a collection of Audley Harrison
memorabilia from eBay. I knew it was
authentic when he threw the towel in.

MASAI GRAHAM

. . . .

A lot of boxers think about their hair during fights. Sometimes they think they'd like it short but then also consider hair extensions. They don't know whether to bob or weave.

IAIN MACDONALD

....

There was confusion at the boxing last night when I asked the guy on the door, 'Is this the way in?'

TONY COWARDS

....

My wrestling partner said, 'Look, I think I've got a sweat rash in the shape of you.' I said, 'We need to talc.'

DARREN WALSH

....

Croatia chooses its prime minister with a boxing match, which usually goes to a Split decision.

LAURA MONMOTH

....

I'm a lover not a fighter, which is why my boxing career ended in scandal.

TONY COWARDS

....

I'm going to Thailand to learn boxing. Mustn't forget my jabs.

DARREN WALSH

....

The French have named a mushroom after Muhammad Ali. They reckon it's the greatest *champignon* of all time.

MASAI GRAHAM

. . . .

I bought a new CD entitled *How to Train Like a Boxer* but when I put it into the sound system, it kept skipping.

SEAN HEGARTY

. . . .

Got a boxing virus on my computer and now my operating system is Linux Lewis.

GRAHAM MUSK

. . . .

I borrowed a Robin Williams' DVD from a friend but gave him the wrong one back. We fought over it for a while but eventually I gave him the right *Hook*.

LAURA MONMOTH

. . . .

I'm into insect boxing – flyweight.

KEVIN HUDSON

. . . .

I've become hooked on watching the injuries sustained by athletes during their matches. It's a crippling addiction.

PAUL SAVAGE

. . . .

Where does a boxer get his shopping? Spar.

SEAN HEGARTY

. . . .

A cash-strapped boxing venue was begging for
patrons to phone in and pledge money for
new equipment. So, I gave them a ring.

HENRY DAWE

. . . .

Mike Tyson was one of the best heavyweights ever.
Whereas Mike Dyson sucked.

NIGEL LOVELL

. . . .

When my parents abandoned me, I was taken in
by a family of marionettes who taught me basic
acrobatics and circus skills. It was a tough life
but I learnt to roll with the Punches.

SEAN PATRICK

. . . .

I was worried about going to the pub after my boxing
match. But I felt better once I'd got the first round in.

PAULINE EYRE

. . . .

What headline should a sports journalist use when
reporting on the previous evening's boxing contest?
A BOUT LAST NIGHT.

HENRY DAWE

. . . .

MUSIC

I took a naked selfie while I made some fresh music the other day, it was a full-frontal new ditty.

RICHARD WOOLFORD

....

I got in trouble when I put my favourite grime artist in a mug. It was a Stormzy in a teacup.

ADELE CLIFF

....

The Beach Boys were always generous with getting the beers in. I'd offer to get them, but they'd always insist, 'I'll get a round, get a round'.

RICHARD PULSFORD

....

Hey, James Brown, when you're making a stew, how well do you take the skin off the vegetables? I peel good!

COLIN LEGGO

....

'I hate Bono and his band.'

'What, you too?'

RICHARD PULSFORD

....

I went to a piano concert in a nightclub recently, saw some incredible fingering.

ADELE CLIFF

....

I hear Neil Diamond has already had three of his five fruit 'n' veg portions again: swede, carrot, lime.

RICHARD PULSFORD

....

Went birdwatching with Sinéad O'Connor, so far it's been seven owls and fifteen jays.

CHRIS NORTON WALKER

....

The best way to listen to music has always been vinyl since records began.

PHILIP SIMON

....

My partner left me to join a Roxette tribute band in Kent. It must've been love, but it's Dover now.

KAT MOLINARI

....

I asked my dad some advice on buying a sound system. He said, 'Panasonic are useless, Hitachi are unreliable, but you can't wrong with a Sony.' I said, 'Dad, these are just stereo types.'

MASAI GRAHAM

....

I hear Liam Gallagher has formed a band with a bunch of terrorists, they're called O-Isis.

RICHARD WOOLFORD

....

I just booked tickets for Ed Sheeran. I was like, 'Next time, do it yourself, you lazy git!'

PHILIP SIMON

....

I was asked to control the sound at an Ed Sheeran concert. I turned it down.

SEAN HEGARTY

....

When you need a country music star in a hurry and have no time to make a costume, you have to call a tailor, swift.

IAIN MACDONALD

....

I had the song 'Orinoco Flow' stuck in my head for days. So, I went to the doctor who diagnosed an Enyarysm.

LAURA MONMOTH

....

I don't like it when folk musicians write angry break-up songs about their ex-girlfriends. It promotes violins against women.

KAT MOLINARI

....

There has been a priceless piece of art stolen by the Steve Miller band. They took the Monet and ran.

CHRIS NORTON WALKER

....

How do Paul Weller and the Jam spend their time at birthday parties? Eating trifles, eating trifles!

COLIN LEGGO

....

My favourite musical is the one about the woman with no depth perception. Miss Eye Gone.

ROB THOMAS

....

Erasure quite like Wheatus's version of 'A Little Respect', which is surprising because they usually try to diss covers.

FRIZ FRIZZLE

....

My stomach gets upset and criticises me every time I perform in a talent contest. I must be suffering from irritable Cowell syndrome.

STEVIE VEGAS

....

Hairdresser: What do you think of your haircut?
Paul McCartney: Love me do!

JOSEPH MURPHY

....

My new musical is sweeping the West End!
Sorry not musical, job.

ROB THOMAS

....

I don't own *19*, *21* or *25*. There's never
Adele moment in our house.

ANDREW TYMMS

....

It's a little-known fact that Elton John doesn't
like iceberg lettuce, he's a rocket man.

TONY COWARDS

....

Beastie Boys have decided to publish our latest
report without giving me a credit. They are very
welcome to parts B and C, but I'm gonna
fight for the right to part A.

STEVIE VEGAS

....

I bought Bob Marley's old printer.
It was good, but it kept jamming.

JOSEPH MURPHY

....

My father plays the tuba, but a little hesitantly.
He's my oompah-pah.

ANDREW TYMMS

....

Mick Jagger used to be a taxi driver for supermodels. He would pick up the likes of Naomi Campbell and Heidi Klum but he never got to pick up the one he really wanted. A rolling stone gathers no Moss.

IAIN MACDONALD

....

I only buy vinyl, for the record.

LOVDEV BARPAGA

....

My favourite band is Division Joy. It's the same band, I just put them in a new order.

MASAI GRAHAM

....

Logarithms, the music that lumberjacks listen to.

TONY COWARDS

....

Someone offered me a loud stereo, but I turned it down.

DARREN WALSH

....

My mum got thrown out of a Kenny Rogers' concert recently for running up onstage and hugging him during one of his songs. I was so angry as I specifically told her beforehand ... you got to know when to hold him.

SEAN HEGARTY

....

I used to work in a cheesecake factory with the singer from Technotronic. His job was to pump up the jam.

LEO KEARSE

....

Does anyone else think that Jim Morrison's wife ever referred to her husband as 'him in Doors'?

GRAHAM MUSK

....

I hate people who play low-frequency guitars. I'm bassist.

DARREN WALSH

....

While I was in Wales I had the lyrics to 'Dancing Queen' tattooed across the breadth of my forearm. I got it done in Abba wrist-width.

LAURA MONMOTH

....

BREAKING NEWS: Beyoncé's husband falls over. Oopsie Jay-Z.

GRAHAM MUSK

....

Did you hear about the affair between the famous violinist and the conductor? Rumour has it she was just stringing him along.

JENAN YOUNIS

....

My favourite band is the one full of
WWI German cooks: the Kaiser Chefs.

KEVIN HUDSON

....

My current project is a comedy-drama about Tears for
Fears. Every critic can independently come up with
the review, 'I find it kinda funny, I find it kinda sad'.

PAUL SAVAGE

....

Back in the nineteenth century a lot of the top
composers got into trouble for plagiarising other
people's music. In particular, Liszt was ticked off.

HENRY DAWE

....

People who listen to my mixtape often get a bad rap.

PAUL SAVAGE

....

'Would you like to see the Bootleg Beatles band?'
'Certainly – they were dreadful last year.'

HENRY DAWE

....

'What's your favourite type of programming
operator, Mrs Parton?'
'Boolean, Boolean, Boolean Boo-le-ee-an.'

SEAN PATRICK

....

There's a little grub in my garden that's annoying me so much. Keeps singing that 'Baby Shark Dance' song. Eventually I called him over and said, ''ere, worm, shut up!'

PAULINE EYRE

....

'Is that AC/DC shouting for a cab?'

'Nah, they're Van Halen!'

'Is that AC/DC hailing for a van?'

FRIZ FRIZZLE

....

Whenever I travel abroad and call my mum, I dial the number and sing, 'It's +44 time!'

PAULINE EYRE

....

What is a brass musician's favourite hobby? Tuba diving.

JENAN YOUNIS

....

BAKING

I found some dreadlocks in a piece of cake,
it was a ragga muffin.

LOVDEV BARPAGA

. . . .

When *The Great British Bake Off* judges disqualified
me for putting Lurpak in the oven, I looked at
them as if butter wouldn't melt.

MASAI GRAHAM

. . . .

When I told them that I'd baked the world's
largest cake, all my neighbours scoffed at it.

TONY COWARDS

. . . .

Tried writing some puns about pizza but
found it really difficult, luckily my Punjabi
friend Deepan helped me out.

LOVDEV BARPAGA

. . . .

In secondary school, I was diagnosed with a
learning difficulty associated with numeracy.
My classmates cheered me right up though,
by baking me a delicious batch of thirteens.

SEAN HEGARTY

. . . .

I tried to make a cake with a cherry on top,
but I couldn't bake well.

MASAI GRAHAM

....

Lost my wallet in the sliced bread section of the
bakery. I went through thick and thin getting it back.

DARREN WALSH

....

Everyone is buying my stolen doughnuts,
they're selling like hot cakes.

TONY COWARDS

....

There's only one way to raid a bakery: all buns glazing.

DARREN WALSH

....

How do you make Apple crumble? Invest in Microsoft.

JOSEPH MURPHY

....

I've always thought that all jokes about oven
temperatures work to a degree.

ADELE CLIFF

....

Channel 4 should make a programme where couples
compete for the worst COVID-19 symptoms, they
should call it *The Great British Bae Cough*.

RICHARD PULSFORD

....

I know a baker who uses a gardening tool,
he's raking in the dough.

RICHARD WOOLFORD

. . . .

The other day I was looking out the corner of my
eye and all I could see were balls of choux pastry,
covered in chocolate with cream in the middle.
I was using my profiterole-vision.

COLIN LEGGO

. . . .

Bakers, eh? They're so kneady.

RICHARD WOOLFORD

. . . .

The last batch of cakes I made required whiskers.
My cat wasn't best pleased.

KAT MOLINARI

. . . .

I baked a cake with Viagra in it,
it was a cock-alert sponge.

ADELE CLIFF

. . . .

When Colin the Caterpillar cake reaches its
use-by date, does it turn into a mushy
chrysalis then a butterfly?

STEVIE VEGAS

. . . .

I recently decorated a cake to look like a
cartoon character dressed as an English queen.
It was a Victoria Spongebob.

KAT MOLINARI

. . . .

Told Paul Hollywood a joke about my broken
proving draw but it didn't get a rise.

CHRIS NORTON WALKER

. . . .

Thanks to my dyslexia I had to get the baking
instructions for meringue read out to me
line by line. What a pavlova!

RICHARD PULSFORD

. . . .

I like to wear an old ladies' French hat
when I'm baking. It's my Mary Beret.

COLIN LEGGO

. . . .

I put my hair in a bun yesterday.
It tasted horrible.

STEVIE VEGAS

. . . .

Chocolate sandwich cookies are only made
in one of two Brazilian cities. Now, I can't
remember if it's São Paulo Oreo de Janeiro.

GRAHAM MUSK

. . . .

For my showstopper I made a sourdough convict,
he was a bread man walking.

CHRIS NORTON WALKER

. . . .

My bakery closed. I failed to do an
adequate whisk assessment.

JOSEPH MURPHY

. . . .

I grew up in the basement of a Warburtons factory.
You could say we lived below the bread line.

ANDREW TYMMS

. . . .

The other day I saw a tissue fondling a crumpet.
It was just a bit of hanky pancake.

IAIN MACDONALD

. . . .

My mum bought me a new sandwich toaster
for Christmas but I still use my old one.
Better the Breville you know.

KEVIN HUDSON

. . . .

I'm just trying to remember the name of the baked
treat my mum made that came with jam and
clotted cream. No, sorry ... it's scone.

SEAN HEGARTY

. . . .

Have you heard that Greggs are designing a new shortcrust pastry with a radish, fish and hazelnut filling? Someone has been given pietic licence.

IAIN MACDONALD

....

When I was in prison my friend said he'd bake me a cake with a surprise in it. I didn't realise I'd swallowed a file till it was tool ate.

GRAHAM MUSK

....

I've made a special dish for my grandfather's funeral. It's a cortège pie.

ANDREW TYMMS

....

I was watching *The Great British Bake Off* when a contestant made a cake shaped like a toilet. I wanted to know the recipe, and thankfully at the end of the episode the presenter told us to find out, we need to phone the Bake-a-Loo line.

LAURA MONMOTH

....

On Easter Sunday, after rising from the tomb, Jesus went out, met people and broke bread with them, proving that breakfast is the most important meal of the deity.

PAUL SAVAGE

....

I tried to make pancakes from watching
a video tutorial online, but I lost interest
as the cook waffled on.

JENAN YOUNIS

· · · · · · · · · · · · · · · · · · · ·

I bake every day, Monday to Friday,
since I completed Couch to 5 Cakes.

KEVIN HUDSON

· · · · · · · · · · · · · · · · · · · ·

The former presenters of *The Great British Bake Off*
have opened a specialist dessert shop off the coast
of Biscay in Spain. It's a Mel and Sue bay.

LAURA MONMOTH

· · · · · · · · · · · · · · · · · · · ·

Oh, you think you've got a way of
making bread rise more? Prove it.

PAUL SAVAGE

· · · · · · · · · · · · · · · · · · · ·

I made some tiny cakes for Jade, Perrie and
Leigh-Anne. I couldn't be bothered to make
them from scratch, so I used a little mix.

PAULINE EYRE

· · · · · · · · · · · · · · · · · · · ·

As the famous vegan saying goes,
'You can't make an omelette.'

FRIZ FRIZZLE

· · · · · · · · · · · · · · · · · · · ·

Ask anyone in the baking trade and they will tell you that their five favourite films are *Carve Her Name with Mother's Pride, Loaf Actually, Ocean's Leaven, Oh! What a Lovely Warburtons* and *Scone with the Wind*.

HENRY DAWE

....

I love pizza, but where I live we have too many pizzerias. Six months ago, we had seven branches of Domino's on our high street, but then one went and now there are none.

NIGEL LOVELL

....

'What are you up to at the moment, Sean?'

'Well, I've got my fingers in a lot of pies.'

'I can see that. Get the fuck out of my bakery.'

SEAN PATRICK

....

'I've glazed those ice buns like you asked, Mary.'

'Don't interrupt, girl – can't you see I'm busy with a customer? I mean, really, I'm trying to serve this lady and you come in here, all buns glazing.'

HENRY DAWE

....

Bloody Black Lace – they might know about singing, but they know nothing about baking! I've just had them on the phone asking, 'What does an AGA do?'

SEAN PATRICK

....

If you put all the jokes in this book into a tin and cooked them in the oven, you'd have a cheesecake.

PAULINE EYRE

....

CINEMA

When I watched the *Star Wars* films for the first time,
I kept getting Chewbacca and the Wampa mixed up.
It was a Wookiee mistake.

KAT MOLINARI

. . . .

I hear that while on the set of *Grease,*
the cast were practising their veterinary skills.
Apparently Olivia neutered John.

COLIN LEGGO

. . . .

Went to a singles' fancy-dress event.
The theme was Liam Neeson films,
all the attractive people were taken.

CHRIS NORTON WALKER

. . . .

What do you see when the Tin Man shouts
into the cold air? A silver scream.

KAT MOLINARI

. . . .

*The Girl with the Dragon Tattoo. The Girl Who Played
with Fire. The Girl Who Kicked the Hornet's Nest.*
Hadn't her parents heard of the naughty step?

ROB THOMAS

. . . .

I managed to swallow the entire DVD
boxset of James Bond, then got the
living daylights kicked out of me.

STEVIE VEGAS

. . . .

When I was a struggling actor, I got this role where
I had to spank Dwayne Johnson. I'd hit rock bottom.

COLIN LEGGO

. . . .

I got fired from my job as a film director.
I tried to leave without making a scene.

JOSEPH MURPHY

. . . .

Déjà Vue. The feeling that you've been
to this cinema before.

TONY COWARDS

. . . .

Been watching all of Keanu Reeves' early nineties
films in chronological order. Don't worry,
I'll soon be up to *Speed*.

STEVIE VEGAS

. . . .

'Always watch Biblical epics in
widescreen' – Sony 16:9

JOSEPH MURPHY

. . . .

Arguments defending Woody Allen are like the women Woody Allen dates. They're not developed enough to be legal.

PAUL SAVAGE

....

I didn't sleep very well last night. I kept getting woken up by the sound of sliding doors. I think I'm being haunted by a Paltrowgeist.

ANDREW TYMMS

....

I went to the Harry Potter pound shop. Everything was a quid each.

KEVIN HUDSON

....

The Hollywood director with the worst personal hygiene was Alfred Itchcock.

RICHARD PULSFORD

....

Who's the best black-and-white, silent comedy, terrorist duo? Laurel and Ji-Hardy.

RICHARD WOOLFORD

....

I have just been cast in a new version of *The Full Monty*. I can't say too much at this stage, but all will be revealed!

ANDREW TYMMS

....

Last time I went to the cinema I saw a trailer
for Battersea Dogs & Cats Home, it was
in full surround hound.

ADELE CLIFF

. . . .

I just watched a crow in a British comedy film.
What a carrion.

RICHARD PULSFORD

. . . .

I was telling these really inappropriate jokes to ghosts.
I've got a sixth sense of humour.

IAIN MACDONALD

. . . .

Turns out *Thor* is not the follow-up to *Frozen*.

CHRIS NORTON WALKER

. . . .

I made an independent movie last year called
The Traffic Warden, but it flopped at the box office.
Turned out, nobody wanted a ticket.

SEAN HEGARTY

. . . .

I went on a date where all we did was discuss
Dick Van Dyke films and then have sex.
Chatty chatty, bang bang.

ADELE CLIFF

. . . .

Putting my *Finding Nemo* costume on
every day is wearing a little fin.

MASAI GRAHAM

....

I always ejaculate when I think about Pennywise
the Dancing Clown. Come to think of it.

IAIN MACDONALD

....

I don't see the point of IMAX cinemas, then again
I've never been able to see the bigger picture.

TONY COWARDS

....

They're making a documentary about a cure for
arthritis. It's called *Silence of the Limbs*.

DARREN WALSH

....

Where does Sebastian from *The Little Mermaid*
put his Christmas presents? Under the tree.

MASAI GRAHAM

....

They're remaking a famous eighties sci-fi film where a
man becomes trapped in a computer simulation, but
this time it's in space. Jeff Bridges is unavailable so
they're looking for a new *Tron* star.

LAURA MONMOTH

....

When I was a lecturer at Warner Brothers Studios, I taught 'I saw a puddy tat'.

DARREN WALSH

....

Pierce Brosnan forgot to get rid of the grey in his hair on Monday, so he had to dye another day.

KEVIN HUDSON

....

To help get more work as a chiropractor, I made a movie and only released tickets for the front row.

SEAN HEGARTY

....

I went to watch a movie about BDSM. I asked, 'Does this have subtitles?' 'Yes. Worm. Maggot. You pathetic little creature. That sort of thing.'

PAUL SAVAGE

....

My great-grandfather, sick of silent films and missing his native Devon coast, finally, at the age of seventy-five, got to see the Torquay he had so longed for.

HENRY DAWE

....

Mad that there are eight *Harry Potter* films with wizards doing attacking spells and no one ever quips that they're going on a charms offensive.

PAUL SAVAGE

....

If you ever wondered what became of the real Butch Cassidy and the Sundance Kid, they've got a nice little business selling German cars. Look them up, they're called Audi Partners.

SEAN PATRICK

....

It's funny how words can have a different meaning from one language to another, isn't it? Like chauffeur. In French, it means anyone who drives a car for someone else. Whereas in English, it's where Sean Connery used to sit while he was watching the TV.

SEAN PATRICK

....

I once watched a Bill Murray film in Greek, but I found that some of the phrases didn't really work. *Lost in Translation*.

NIGEL LOVELL

....

That guy from *The Dark Knight* got arrested, but the people from his church got him out. They posted Christian Bale.

PAULINE EYRE

....

OPERA

A Russian male pianist with breasts, who I had affectionately named Rack Man kept annoying me, so I shouted, 'Rack man! Enough!'

JOSEPH MURPHY

....

I thought 'Nessun Dorma' was sang by Guy Garvey! Turns out I don't know my arias from my Elbow.

PHILIP SIMON

....

My friend does security at the local opera, he's the Nessun doorman.

ADELE CLIFF

....

My friend wants to totally change his opera singing style from castrato to bass, sadly though he just doesn't have the balls.

RICHARD WOOLFORD

....

I hear there's an American chat show host that keeps being sang to by a ghost in a mask ... Phantom of the Oprah.

COLIN LEGGO

....

The largest opera singer is a woman of some aria.

RICHARD PULSFORD

. . . .

My friend went from starring in opera comedies to working in a nail salon. She's always been a *buffa*.

KAT MOLINARI

. . . .

I really enjoyed going to the opera.
It had a *Carmen* effect on me.

RICHARD PULSFORD

. . . .

My single female friend wrote a musical,
It Ain't Over till The Cat Lady Sings.

CHRIS NORTON WALKER

. . . .

There's a new BBC Radio 4 show where classical musicians have to play without hesitation, deviation or repetition for sixty seconds. *Just a Minuet.*

ADELE CLIFF

. . . .

Being in the orchestra for an opera, it's the pits.

CHRIS NORTON WALKER

. . . .

I've written an opera about training at a crispbread factory in Liverpool. It's called *Educating Ryvita*.

ROB THOMAS

. . . .

Rihanna asked if she was required to do opera
in order to be signed by her record label.
They said, 'It's not *obbligato*, Ri.'

KAT MOLINARI

....

The first rule of opera club is to
state your aria of expertise.

STEVIE VEGAS

....

I've written an opera that's anti-sexist and anti-
fat-shaming. It's called *It Ain't Over Till the Person Sings*.

ROB THOMAS

....

I recently wrote a musical about a can of
fizzy orange that wears a facemask.
It's called *The Fanta of the Opera*.

SEAN HEGARTY

....

What do you call an opera singer who suffers
from impotence? Fláccido Domingo.

TONY COWARDS

....

Have you heard about the new musical based
on the life of an American chat show host?
The Phantom of the Oprah.

ANDREW TYMMS

....

**What do you call an Italian family of opera lovers?
The sopranos.**

JENAN YOUNIS

. . . .

**The very first operas written in around 1600
really were a Baroque through.**

IAIN MACDONALD

. . . .

**If anyone is looking for a harpist,
I'm sure I can pull a few strings.**

STEVIE VEGAS

. . . .

**I got kicked out of the opera for apparently being
a gangster. I was just copying the sopranos.**

MASAI GRAHAM

. . . .

**How did I feel about Pavarotti singing my name?
I was composed.**

MASAI GRAHAM

. . . .

Brian Eno's full name is Brian English National Opera.

TONY COWARDS

. . . .

**I can't stop singing arias all day long.
They've really got under my skin, like opera ticks.**

PAULINE EYRE

. . . .

What about that opera where Sylvester Stallone presents a big jug of beer that costs just a bit more than 99¢? *The Rocky Dollar Pitcher Show*.

IAIN MACDONALD

....

Every time I come home, I wipe my feet on a picture of Pavarotti. It's a Nessun Dormat!

SEAN HEGARTY

....

I've bought the Phantom of the Opera a special Christmas gift this year. I can't wait to see his face.

GRAHAM MUSK

....

The opera singer most likely to eat flatbreads was Luciano Havearoti

LAURA MONMOTH

....

Got kicked out a restaurant for trying to stage an opera. He said, 'Sir, you are making a scene.'

PAUL SAVAGE

....

The kids were excited when I suggested going to the playground. Less so when we arrived at the theatre for the play *Ground*, a sober reflection of dirt and earth.

PAUL SAVAGE

....

I went to see The Three Tenors. Cost me five tenners.

KEVIN HUDSON

....

Benjamin's mother always insisted that her son should look well groomed when out and about in public. She took it upon herself to keep Britten tidy.

HENRY DAWE

....

I'm not saying my mate Geoff is uncultured but when I asked him if he wanted to come to *La traviata* with me, he said, 'I don't like Italian restaurants.'

NIGEL LOVELL

....

I took anti-flatulence pills before I went to see *Madame Butterfly*. I was trying to keep my opera wind-free.

KEVIN HUDSON

....

I'm not saying my mate Geoff is uncultured but when I asked him if he liked *Don Giovanni*, he said, 'I don't like ice cream.'

NIGEL LOVELL

....

Saw a musical recently that was simultaneously the best and worst thing I've ever seen. It was *Schrodinger's Cats*.

SEAN PATRICK

....

Which donkey is the subject of an opera based
on an original novel by Miguel de Cervantes?
Don Quixote.

HENRY DAWE

....

I run an opera company. I love working out
the profits at the end of the show. I'll count
a tenner, then another tenner ...

PAULINE EYRE

....

Why is *Carmen* the best opera ever?
Because the composer was so Bizet perfecting it.

JENAN YOUNIS

....

EXERCISE

My gym is a mix of serious exercisers and bored
gossipers. You look around the room and it's like,
'Run ... rabbit ... run ... rabbit ... run run run'.

PHILIP SIMON

....

I used to paint while on the exercise bikes.
I thought my northern personal trainer said,
'Keep yer art rate up.'

KAT MOLINARI

....

I've given up on personal fitness consultants.
My bum actually looks bigger in running gear
now – thanks to my added-ass trainers.

RICHARD PULSFORD

....

I took martial arts classes in a Catholic church and one
of the sisters there let me throw her across the room
to practise. I was working on my nun chucks.

KAT MOLINARI

....

My dad's mum keeps running off during our
weekly yoga sessions. Nana stay.

ADELE CLIFF

....

If you ask an Australian Buddhist to
move they'll reply, 'Nah, 'm stay.'

CHRIS NORTON WALKER

. . . .

I fired my personal trainer for saying I
could lose weight just by standing still.
I told him it wasn't working out.

PHILIP SIMON

. . . .

I'm a very meticulous amputee, I always like
to make sure my prosthetic leg fits properly.
The other day I was out jogging and it came
loose. I was kicking myself!

COLIN LEGGO

. . . .

I turned up for kickboxing class today, forgetting
it was cancelled. I could have kicked myself.

RICHARD PULSFORD

. . . .

To exercise I like to knock on all of the doors
in the local area – Jehovah's Fitness.

CHRIS NORTON WALKER

. . . .

I don't like to brag but I can control
a kayak brilliantly. Canoe?

ADELE CLIFF

. . . .

On my first day at the gym, I was given a gun
and sent out to shoot Nazis in the woods.
Not how I'd imagined resistance training.

PHILIP SIMON

. . . .

When my local gym removed all their windows,
everyone stayed the same weight. No pane, no gain.

COLIN LEGGO

. . . .

My parents were fitness freaks. If I misbehaved,
they made me do naughty-step aerobics.

ROB THOMAS

. . . .

My aim is to run a marathon in six months.
That's only about 0.145 miles a day, so it
could be quite achievable.

STEVIE VEGAS

. . . .

Decided that my footwear isn't strong enough.
I'm going to have to send them to boot camp.

STEVIE VEGAS.

. . . .

I decided to eat a curry halfway through a marathon.
It was a bad decision in the long run.

DARREN WALSH

. . . .

I just did a hundred press-ups.
The lift was slow and I was impatient.

JOSEPH MURPHY

....

I'm jealous of my friends who've got personal trainers.
Oh, to go for a jog without having to borrow a pair!

ROB THOMAS

....

I saw an advert for a new yoga class. £100 a session.
I thought, 'I can't stretch to that.'

ANDREW TYMMS

....

The Brighton and London marathon promoters
are enemies. It's a long running feud.

JOSEPH MURPHY

....

My personal fitness coach is absolutely furious
with my lack of progress. She's my cross trainer.

ANDREW TYMMS

....

Have you heard about the Mexican bodybuilder
that ran out of protein shakes? No Whey José.

IAIN MACDONALD

....

If you're struggling to do pull-ups at the gym, chin up.

TONY COWARDS

....

Under the government guidance of opening pools,
I've been keeping to the two-metre pool.

LOVDEV BARPAGA

. . . .

I had a poker night with my Weight Watchers group
but none of them would put their chips down.

MASAI GRAHAM

. . . .

There were these two very well-to-do women
who would meet socially around midday to go
to the gym. They were ladies who lunge.

IAIN MACDONALD

. . . .

My carbohydrate diet isn't going well. I tried to
steal some spaghetti from my mum's house but
she saw me, and I couldn't get pasta.

MASAI GRAHAM

. . . .

My Pakistani friend is taking self-defence classes.
He calls it Karachi.

LOVDEV BARPAGA

. . . .

A sign outside a pub showing the women's
World Cup final said '22 WOMEN, 1 CUP'. I thought,
That sequel's got a bigger production value.

LEO KEARSE

. . . .

I was walking down the street when someone hit me with a sweet-smelling, burning stick. I was incensed!

LEO KEARSE

....

I was riding my bike when the steering went. I took it to the bike shop and when I picked it up, the brakes failed. I've got to get off this vicious cycle.

PAULINE EYRE

....

Went on a date with a gym instructor.
It didn't work out.

DARREN WALSH

....

Off to the gym dressed as Satan,
need to exorcise my demons.

TONY COWARDS

....

Recently, I went to the gym dressed as a clown.
Turns out, it was a beginner circuits class.

SEAN HEGARTY

....

My wife used to be a burlesque dancer around the North West – it kept her fit. She's given it up now – couldn't be doing wi' tassel.

EL BALDINHO

....

I didn't do well in my Army fitness test,
but I managed to pass out.

EL BALDINHO

. . . .

I'm so fit and can pull my foot so far up behind me
that my ankle touches the back of my thigh.
Actually, that's a bit of a stretch.

GRAHAM MUSK

. . . .

I've got two personal trainers. One for each foot.

SEAN HEGARTY

. . . .

I once ran in a Decathlon. It took ages for the
security guards to throw me out.

LAURA MONMOTH

. . . .

I go running every Saturday morning dressed
as a Mod. Everyone does – it's parkarun.

KEVIN HUDSON

. . . .

In my attempt to spend 2020 getting fitter
I ordered a fitness tracker off Wish and was
expecting something really good for my money,
but I ended up only getting a Bitfit.

GRAHAM MUSK

. . . .

They say after exercising, you should do a long
stretch, so I've been sentenced to seven years for GBH.

PAUL SAVAGE

. . . .

My mum insisted that I do more exercise,
so she bought me a treadmill. She also
got me a football to boot.

HENRY DAWE

. . . .

I gained a lot of weight in lockdown.
Turns out that I could go big and go home.

PAUL SAVAGE

. . . .

People ask me where I get my ideas from. Well, every
morning I go for a run and take a notepad with me.
I say notepad, it's more of an exercise book.

NIGEL LOVELL

. . . .

I've just heard that my grandmother has died.
She was abseiling at the time and her equipment
failed. So, in one way, it was a release.

SEAN PATRICK

. . . .

'Will you please welcome Mr and Mrs Comes-In-
Handy-At-The-Sports-Centre and their son Jim-Kit.'

HENRY DAWE

. . . .

EXERCISE

My personal trainer made me do so many
abdominal exercises, I wanted to curl up and die.

PAULINE EYRE

....

I started playing badminton to get into shape,
it didn't work because I hit a brick wall.

JENAN YOUNIS

....

TRAVEL

LEICESTER

UCAS wanted me to send them information on where
I plan to study in Leicester, so I said, 'I'll DMU.'

ADELE CLIFF

....

Every time an epidemiologist says, 'It's imperative
that we "flatten the curve"', I imagine the manager
of the Curve Theatre having a panic attack.

RICHARD PULSFORD

....

Leicester City's Jamie Vardy keeps running into
brides and grooms on their big day. It's worth
going just to see his wedding tackle.

PHILIP SIMON

....

I want to grow marijuana for a living.
You know, get a job in the high fields.

KAT MOLINARI

....

Leicester was founded on the Roman road between
Exeter and Lincoln but, for a long time, people
didn't know what the Fosse was about.

RICHARD PULSFORD

....

My satnav failed while I was driving from Leicester
to Sheffield and I got tied up in Notts.

CHRIS NORTON WALKER

....

There's a bear that lives in the M1
motorway services: Leicester Forest Beast.

CHRIS NORTON WALKER

....

It would be great to have trams back in Leicester. I'd
bounce all over the city. They'd call me Tram Pauline.

PAULINE EYRE

....

I discovered the Chief Editor of the *Leicester
Mercury* lying motionless on the floor. I phoned
999 and was asked to check his circulation. I broke
into his office, did some digging around, and
was able to let the operator know that he'd
only sold nine copies that week.

STEVIE VEGAS

....

I always carry a spare tyre when driving around
the city Leicester problem should arise.

HENRY DAWE

....

Is the local plumber Leicester Spigot?

PAULINE EYRE

....

When I bought the train ticket using a £20 note, they said, 'Change at Leicester.' I stood firm and insisted they give me the change right there, right then.

STEVIE VEGAS

....

When I found out Heskey had bigger feet than me I thought, 'Try walking, Emile, in my shoes.'

MASAI GRAHAM

....

My driving instructor knows how to position a car, she taught me some great new parks.

KAT MOLINARI

....

Jonny Evans won't hear anything said against the local shopping centre. He likes to defend the high cross.

IAIN MACDONALD

....

Can I do puns about Leicester City midfielders? Yes, Ndidi.

TONY COWARDS

....

Richard the Third was so named because he didn't do very well at university, unlike his sister Elizabeth the First and younger brother, Desmond Tutu.

TONY COWARDS

....

A Plantagenet king extended his bank loan.
It was Richard Deferred.

MASAI GRAHAM

. . . .

I went into the National Space Centre recently. I'll tell
you what, they were right. There's loads of room in it.

SEAN HEGARTY

. . . .

Since a former jockey moved to the area, the city
has become a lot more left wing. Leicester Pivot.

LAURA MONMOTH

. . . .

I received a surprise invite to a dinner dance at the
theatre in Leicester. That was a Curve ball.

KEVIN HUDSON

. . . .

If you're less outgoing than the
other guy, are you Leicestershire?

PAULINE EYRE

. . . .

De Montfort Hall always get their marketing out
early so they can be ahead of the Curve.

HENRY DAWE

. . . .

The most famous lake in Leicester is Loch Down.

KEVIN HUDSON

. . . .

Who was Leicester City's cheesiest player?
Peter Stilton.

NIGEL LOVELL

. . . .

I thought I'd stolen money in Leicester recently,
from just a random person. Turns out it's
Jamie Vardy's account!

SEAN HEGARTY

. . . .

Do you call the local racist Leicester Bigot?

PAULINE EYRE

. . . .

EUROPE

The Roman emperor's wife hates playing hide and seek because wherever she goes Julius Caesar.

ADELE CLIFF

....

I've been invited to Switzerland to host a new game show sponsored by Dignitas called *Take Me Out*.

PHILIP SIMON

....

Russia is having a closing down sale.
Everything Moscow.

RICHARD PULSFORD

....

Which European country was named after its oar-based sport fanaticism? Row-mania.

RICHARD WOOLFORD

....

Pardon is the only French word that I know.
I can only apologise.

MASAI GRAHAM

....

Some European countries are mean, others Armenia.

ADELE CLIFF

....

My friend from Bolton was offered the chance
to move to Scandinavia with her boyfriend
but she declined and told him 'Norway'.

KAT MOLINARI

. . . .

You can keep up with all the action for
Germany's National Marijuana Day
by following their #HashTag.

PHILIP SIMON

. . . .

My workplace tried to transfer to France
but I was Avignon of it.

KAT MOLINARI

. . . .

The Europeans who take the longest to get the
dust out of their carpets are the Slovaks.

RICHARD PULSFORD

. . . .

My dogs are holidaying in Amsterdam,
bitches be tripping.

CHRIS NORTON WALKER

. . . .

When Brexit happened, I almost removed myself from
Tinder but it's good to be in the singles market.

COLIN LEGGO

. . . .

A man has been run over by a boat in Venice.
I sent my gondolences.

JOSEPH MURPHY

....

The Vatican are selling candy versions
of biblical figures, sweet Jesus!

CHRIS NORTON WALKER

....

My dad was a rebellious French chef.
He taught me never to play by the Rouxs.

ROB THOMAS

....

ME: I'm starting a football team in the
South of France

FRIEND: Toulouse?

ME: No, to win – you weirdo!

SEAN HEGARTY

....

I saw this group of teenagers going to a
Europe-themed fancy-dress party, thinking they
were dressed like Benny from ABBA. Kids these
days, they don't know they're Björn.

COLIN LEGGO

....

When my dad nearly choked to death on
a German sausage, we feared the wurst.

TONY COWARDS

. . . .

In Iceland they have a shop that sells
tepid food called Britain.

ROB THOMAS

. . . .

Only just discovered that Ibiza is in Spain.
Sorry to rave on about it ...

STEVIE VEGAS

. . . .

Why did the cat take his girlfriend to Paris for the
weekend? He wanted to whisk 'er away.

ANDREW TYMMS

. . . .

Brexit is like a catheter for Britain because when
we leave, we will no longer be incontinent.

ROB THOMAS

. . . .

Later on, in the evening, I shall be showing
you a life-size map of Europe.
Let's see how that unfolds.

STEVIE VEGAS

. . . .

I work in a restaurant and Spanish people always order aquatic food — 'Another Juan bites the ducks'.

JOSEPH MURPHY

....

My friend thought that a young frog was a bit German, I thought it was a tad Pole myself.

IAIN MACDONALD

....

Last year, I went on holiday to Spain by myself. I was a Barceloner.

ANDREW TYMMS

....

My dad's dying wish was to have his ashes scattered in Reykjavík and that's why mum's gone to Iceland.

MASAI GRAHAM

....

When travelling to Bulgaria, I spent a night in Sofia. Dorothy, Blanche and Rose were furious.

IAIN MACDONALD

....

I've just bought my skimpy underwear for Eurovision, it's a thong for Europe.

TONY COWARDS

....

My mate thinks all life on earth began 6,000 years ago in Dubrovnik. He's a Croatianist.

LEO KEARSE

....

I saw a bull on a Scottish mountain doing a Japanese poem – it was a high coo.

LEO KEARSE

....

Where in Spain would you go to get a suit tailored? Sevilla Row.

JENAN YOUNIS

....

I just deleted all the German names off my phone. It's Hans-free.

DARREN WALSH

....

My friend keeps setting fire to Belgian detectives. He's a Poirotmaniac.

DARREN WALSH

....

I saw the German prime minister wearing a triangular pubic wig – it's an angular merkin.

LEO KEARSE

....

Brexit can be easily reversed – Tixerb!

EL BALDINHO

....

I used to work in a café. One day this German lady came in. I said, 'Hi, would you like a complimentary biscuit?'

'*Nein*!' she replied.

'Don't be greedy, you can have ONE like everybody else!' I said.

SEAN HEGARTY

....

There's a guy in Wales who was refused a licence to marry a local river. Don't feel sorry for him, it's Taff love.

LAURA MONMOTH

....

Years ago, the Italians traded their castles with the Chinese in return for pasta in a deal known as Penne for Your Forts.

KEVIN HUDSON

....

I'd love to tell you all my favourite French cities, but the list is Toulon.

LAURA MONMOTH

....

My mate Ian is convinced that Russia is in Europe, but I'm sure it's in Asia. I keep saying, 'It's not Europe, Ian!'

PAULINE EYRE

....

Ancient Greek soldiers loved strong-flavoured beers,
except spear carriers, who were hoplite.

PAUL SAVAGE

....

If you're exhausted by work, you should look up
holiday cottages and Bucharest online.

HENRY DAWE

....

In England it's a pack of wild dogs,
but in Germany it's a Wolfgang.

KEVIN HUDSON

....

I couldn't risk going on a walking holiday
in France with my dodgy Pyrenees.

HENRY DAWE

....

I don't mean to boast, but I've had sex with more
fit Italian women than you've had hot donnas.

SEAN PATRICK

....

Do you like puns about French towns? Good, 'cos I've
got Rhiems, which is Nice. Haven't really, Avignon.
That's the trouble with puns about French towns if
you go on Toulon, they can Rouen the joke.

NIGEL LOVELL

....

When it came to negotiating the post-Brexit fishing agreements, both sides just seemed to flounder.

PAULINE EYRE

....

I want to go to Chernobyl, but it's still got unsafe amounts of nuclear fallout, or as I call it 'fission chips'.

PAUL SAVAGE

....

My fiancé proposed in Paris; it was the place where we first met and Eiffel for him.

JENAN YOUNIS

....

SUMMER

My friend has finally learnt his lesson on naked
barbecuing, last time he did it he burnt his sausage!

ADELE CLIFF

. . . .

I hear Jay-Z had to close down his ice-cream
van business, he had 99 problems.

RICHARD WOOLFORD

. . . .

I've taken up carpentry, making wooden mannequins,
and am currently working on my beech body.

KAT MOLINARI

. . . .

Asked my dad how solar panels work,
and he started to explain, 'Son ...'

CHRIS NORTON WALKER

. . . .

I like to rate my sunburn from one to tan.

COLIN LEGGO

. . . .

I wish my neighbours would stop their
loud BBQs, for frying out loud.

CHRIS NORTON WALKER

. . . .

If you suffer with hay fever don't take remedies
from a herbalist. I did and I came out in
chives. What a waste of thyme!

PHILIP SIMON

....

I love putting on really strong sun cream.
I guess it's that feel-good factor.

STEVIE VEGAS

....

The office bullies have taped a calendar to my back.
I thought those days were behind me.

JOSEPH MURPHY

....

Last summer, I went into business looking after
people's cats while they went on holiday, but
financially, it was a disaster. A friend said:
'That cattery will get you nowhere.'

ANDREW TYMMS

....

While Ken jumped to the front of the line for
his sausages and burgers, Barbie queued.

IAIN MACDONALD

....

My mum couldn't hang the last bit of washing on
the line so I had to take her down a peg or two.

MASAI GRAHAM

....

If I owned a travel agency in Birkenhead I'd definitely call it Wirral Going on a Summer Holiday.

TONY COWARDS

. . . .

I won a year's supply of ice cream,
but there was a wafer in the contract.

DARREN WALSH

. . . .

My new girlfriend reminds me of the summer weather. She's in her mid-twenties, hot and I guarantee that she'll be gone by the autumn!

SEAN HEGARTY

. . . .

On holiday we had naked BBQs,
or as I call them, bare grills.

KEVIN HUDSON

. . . .

World Cups are like orgies. Much more chance of an upset in the early group stages.

PAUL SAVAGE

. . . .

The last job I was offered was with a sun cream manufacturer. They said they were impressed with the way I had applied myself.

RICHARD PULSFORD

. . . .

Somerset: the crowds at Ascot,
Henley and Wimbledon.

HENRY DAWE

....

I can't remember what this joke is about.
Is it the sun? Is it the beach? Is it the blue sky?
Summerthing like that ...

PAULINE EYRE

....

When I want to know if it's hot enough to remove my
clothing at the beach, I listen to the *Stripping Forecast*.

ADELE CLIFF

....

My wife and I found a great way to stay hydrated
during last year's heatwave. It was the Summer of 69s.

PHILIP SIMON

....

I cheated on a Ferris wheel operator last July
and he didn't even dump me, which was
odd because he had fairgrounds to.

KAT MOLINARI

....

My girlfriend is terrible at applying sun cream.
I shouldn't rub it in.

COLIN LEGGO

....

Where do you think I should go on my summer holiday? Answers on a postcard, please!

STEVIE VEGAS

. . . .

Help! The clocks have gone back and I'm having difficulty adjusting my sundial.

JOSEPH MURPHY

. . . .

Last summer, I went on a camping holiday with my girlfriend. We camped on the side of a mountain.

That was an uphill snuggle.

ANDREW TYMMS

. . . .

For people looking at buying holiday homes. Some folks may take out adverts in the likes of the *Guardian* and *The Times*, but what I would recommend is a place in the *Sun*.

IAIN MACDONALD

. . . .

Sunni Muslims always look on the bright side of life.

LOVDEV BARPAGA

. . . .

I once had a summer job cremating policemen. I just wanted to urn a few coppers.

MASAI GRAHAM

. . . .

My family are having an argument about
the seating arrangements for the summer
BBQ, I'm sitting on the fence.

TONY COWARDS

. . . .

Someone went and cleaned out my
drainpipes while I was on holiday. Gutted.

DARREN WALSH

. . . .

I'm taking my family to Sixerife next summer.
I can't afford Tenerife.

SEAN HEGARTY

. . . .

Chuck Berry used to sell hamburgers
in Marrakesh on a Moroccan roll.

KEVIN HUDSON

. . . .

Our holiday in August was a complete
disappointment. Our lad Toby said he was too old
to go away with his parents and refused to join us.
My wife and I were so upset. The whole fortnight
we suffered from Lack of Son Disorder.

HENRY DAWE

. . . .

July-ke my joke about the summer? No? July noted.

PAULINE EYRE

. . . .

WINTER

I tell people it's winter in my bank account
because it's normally sub-zero.

ADELE CLIFF

....

I punched my neighbour after he forced me to grit
his driveway and jump-start his car this morning, and
now I'm the one being arrested for a salt and battery.

RICHARD PULSFORD

....

Why is everyone changing their name to Angelina
this Christmas? 'Tis the season to be Jolie.

RICHARD WOOLFORD

....

Richard III would host insult battles every
Christmas. He'd begin the night by announcing,
'Now is the winter of our diss content.'

KAT MOLINARI

....

Last winter, I went ice skating with my dad's
brother. Unfortunately, he slipped and
that's how I broke my uncle.

ANDREW TYMMS

....

Got a digital map of the best skiing destinations from the Alp Store.

CHRIS NORTON WALKER

. . . .

I gatecrashed the Snowman's wedding party. Talk about a frosty reception.

COLIN LEGGO

. . . .

I really love my de-icer. We certainly get into a lot of scrapes.

STEVIE VEGAS

. . . .

I just took a girl out ice skating. Slammed right into her.

JOSEPH MURPHY

. . . .

Did you know that the world sit-up champion is a yeti? He's known as the Abdominal Snowman.

IAIN MACDONALD

. . . .

Someone knocked on my front door once and when I answered, this guy started asking me if I had a hot-water bottle or electric blanket that I could lend him because he couldn't stop shivering. I shut the door in his face. Damn, I hate those cold callers.

SEAN HEGARTY

. . . .

My daughter wants to become a princess
like Snow White, though her stepmother
is against the idea.

LOVDEV BARPAGA

....

What do you do if the bank freeze your
savings account? Get a de-ISA.

MASAI GRAHAM

....

I've decided to get involved in the snow globe
industry, just to shake things up a little.

TONY COWARDS

....

I used to brush my turkey with seasoning
at work but baste at home now.

DARREN WALSH

....

Each year, I used to look forward to the shortest Day,
but since Doris died they're all quite tall.

LAURA MONMOTH

....

Band Aid are re-releasing their eighties Christmas
song to raise money for blankets for kids in cold
countries. It's called 'Duvet Know It's Christmas?'.

KAT MOLINARI

....

I'm fed up with fake winter weather. That's why I've joined the Campaign for Real Hail.

KEVIN HUDSON

. . . .

'The preparations for the festive season are in full swing, are they?'

'Absolutely.'

'Turkey?'

'No, we're not going abroad this year.'

HENRY DAWE

. . . .

I spent £100 on a warm winter jumper.
I think I got fleeced.

PAULINE EYRE

. . . .

The magician said, 'Think of a number,' so I imagined being out on a really cold day without gloves on.

RICHARD PULSFORD

. . . .

After the accident, my skiing career went downhill fast.

CHRIS NORTON WALKER

. . . .

Just been round to Flo Rida's house, and he's got some new trousers specifically for playing games on Halloween. He's got those apple-bobbing Jeans ...

PAUL SAVAGE

. . . .

I was almost attacked by a melting snowman but I thaw him coming.

COLIN LEGGO

. . . .

My mouth keeps filling up with snow every time I'm about to perform. Guess I'd better grit my teeth and get on with it.

STEVIE VEGAS

. . . .

Someone just stole all my presents. The police have identified a green, furry man as their primary Seuss-pect.

JOSEPH MURPHY

. . . .

How do owls keep warm in winter? Central hooting.

ANDREW TYMMS

. . . .

I saw boxes of sandwiches, pasties and salads all tumbling down a snowy mountain. It was an avalunch.

IAIN MACDONALD

. . . .

I chased Santa out of my house on Christmas Eve.
He said, 'I'm contracted to be here,' and I replied,
'Get out, Claus!'

MASAI GRAHAM

. . . .

Our council couldn't clear the roads of snow
because they were using the grit for medical
purposes – that's just rubbing salt in the wound.

TONY COWARDS

. . . .

I love purchasing bears from the Arctic.
Argh! I hate purchasing bears from the
Arctic. I'm buypolar.

DARREN WALSH

. . . .

I'm thinking of making an app for pirates
that are stuck out at sea over the winter.
It'll be called, Shiver Me Tinders.

SEAN HEGARTY

. . . .

I've booked on an Arctic safari.
They guarantee that you'll see at least
five polar bears. That's the bear minimum.

KEVIN HUDSON

. . . .

My French friend is shying away from the pressures of cooking for his family at Christmas by booking them all into a restaurant. He's something of a Noël Coward.

HENRY DAWE

· · · · · · · · · · · · · · · · · · · ·

I went for a job as a snowscape artist,
but I couldn't get a winter view.

PAULINE EYRE

· · · · · · · · · · · · · · · · · · · ·

SEASIDE

Last week I pulled a muscle,
I'm now banned from the aquarium.

ADELE CLIFF

....

I heard rumours there would be a place to
park my U-boat at the harbour but it turned
out they had no sub stance.

RICHARD PULSFORD

....

I went to this beach where you could see people
having sex with sea life. They looked so happy
because they were releasing in dolphins.
Maybe that's the porpoise.

PHILIP SIMON

....

I hope the waves are high enough to
surf this summer. That'd be swell.

KAT MOLINARI

....

Due to new COVID-19 restrictions,
Brighton is now in Pier 2.

CHRIS NORTON WALKER

....

There has been lots of discussion within the fishing community about the best way to take worms off hooks. It's a huge debait.

COLIN LEGGO

....

Seaweed is really good for you.
If you're ever in trouble, sea kelp.

ROB THOMAS

....

Visited the bottom of the sea with a cartoon dog.
I went Scooby diving!

STEVIE VEGAS

....

What's a dolphin's favourite mobile network operator company? EE.

JOSEPH MURPHY

....

When is the best time to visit a sandy beach? Dune.

ANDREW TYMMS

....

Someone pointed at my drink and said, 'That straw is bad, it's single-use plastic. After you've used it, it'll go into the sea and kill a turtle.'
'In that case, it's not single-use plastic,' I said.

LEO KEARSE

....

How do you know that seaweed,
plankton and sea lettuce are homosexual?
'Cause they're algae.

IAIN MACDONALD

....

I used to be a deep-sea diver but had to quit
though – I couldn't handle the pressure.

TONY COWARDS

....

'Hello, Fishermen's Advice Bureau?'

'Help! I've got a bite, what do I do?!'

'Please hold the line . . .'

DARREN WALSH

....

I thought my dad turned into Arnold Schwarzenegger
on the beach once. Turns out, he just said,
'Oil Me Back!'

SEAN HEGARTY

....

I went litter picking at the beach and got asked
if I could see any rubbish. I said, 'Shore can.'

LAURA MONMOTH

....

We stayed in a guesthouse with a barber shop
on the ground floor. It was Hair BnB.

KEVIN HUDSON

....

Trips to the South Pacific Islands are Atoll protected.

PAUL SAVAGE

....

'Do join me on the beach this Saturday.
They've forecast a nice bright day and I can
bring a picnic to divide up between us.'
'Sounds like a case of Sonny and Cher.'

HENRY DAWE

....

I know you want me to write a joke about
Blackpool or Brighton or the Costa del Sol,
but I'm not going to resort to that.

PAULINE EYRE

....

Sorry I'm late, I was putting an orca into
a SodaStream and got waylaid.

FRIZ FRIZZLE

....

I saw a man doing a poo in the sea. I was going to tell
him off, but I realised it was just a plop in the ocean.

ADELE CLIFF

....

I used to work in a lighthouse. I still get flashbacks.

RICHARD PULSFORD

. . . .

I like fishing on nudist beaches,
it's the best place to get your tackle out.

RICHARD WOOLFORD

. . . .

I hate sandy beaches. I just can't walk normally
with the silly footwear. Philip flops!

PHILIP SIMON

. . . .

My mate wondered why seagulls kept fighting her
and I told her it was the chip on her shoulder.

KAT MOLINARI

. . . .

I stole all of the shells from the beach:
'Quick, the coast is clear!'

CHRIS NORTON WALKER

. . . .

I saw Jay-Z in his ice-cream van at the seaside.
Sadly, all his chocolate flakes had melted.
He's got 99 problems.

COLIN LEGGO

. . . .

I've had enough of the seaside – I'm surf-bored.

KEVIN HUDSON

. . . .

Got a job working for Alan Sugar, building seafaring vessels. It's an apprenticeship.

STEVIE VEGAS

. . . .

'Knock knock knock knock knock knock knock knock.'

'Who's there?'

'Knocktopus the Octopus.'

JOSEPH MURPHY

. . . .

Last time I was on holiday, I went to a wild party in the middle of the ocean. It was a wave.

ANDREW TYMMS

. . . .

Sean Connery went to a pebbled beach and asked, 'Is this a shingle beach?' I replied, 'No, there are married couples here too.'

IAIN MACDONALD

. . . .

I was hoping to read the latest book about people who think their body parts are connected to the seaside, but my hands are tide.

SEAN HEGARTY

. . . .

Where did the Beach Boys get their haircut?
Barber Ann's.

TONY COWARDS

. . . .

I phoned Seaworld's dolphin show hotline, and they
said, 'Calls may be recorded for training porpoises.'
So that's how they do it.

DARREN WALSH

. . . .

It's hard to list the beaches where you hear
the most swearing without a Falmouth.

LAURA MONMOTH

. . . .

I'm absolutely convinced the pandemic will be
over and we'll be able to go to the seaside
this summer. It's a shore thing.

PAULINE EYRE

. . . .

COUNTRYSIDE

In Devon, a dead cow is known as an Exmoor.

RICHARD PULSFORD

. . . .

I rolled around in poo on a farm,
which was very in manure of me.

ADELE CLIFF

. . . .

What bird swings both ways? A bisexu-owl.

RICHARD WOOLFORD

. . . .

I listed my favourite plots of land in
an Excel spreadsheet. I remember when
it were nowt but fields.

PHILIP SIMON

. . . .

I find it relaxing planting spuds in fields.
It's a form of meadow-tating.

KAT MOLINARI

. . . .

Ladbrokes are opening shops in country lanes
for those who want to hedge their bets.

CHRIS NORTON WALKER

. . . .

When I was visiting the countryside,
I was beaten at chess by a small mouse-like
mammal. That was a shrew move.

COLIN LEGGO

· · · · · · · · · · · · · · · · · · · ·

Using semaphore, I have invented a new way to
tell farmers that their favourite stabled animal has
sadly passed away. I've put a lot of time into it,
so I hope I'm not flagging a dead horse.

STEVIE VEGAS

· · · · · · · · · · · · · · · · · · · ·

Shop Assistant: Have you got a store card?

Female Stork: Many times.

JOSEPH MURPHY

· · · · · · · · · · · · · · · · · · · ·

I've written a joke about a fat badger,
but I couldn't fit it into my set.

MASAI GRAHAM

· · · · · · · · · · · · · · · · · · · ·

A mate of mine is a shepherd. Things haven't been
easy for him recently. Ever since he lost his flock,
he's been having sheepless nights.

ANDREW TYMMS

· · · · · · · · · · · · · · · · · · · ·

Trying to identity the sticky liquid from various trees, anyone want to join my WhatSap group?

TONY COWARDS

. . . .

I castrated a sheep. That raised the baa.

DARREN WALSH

. . . .

There is a tree that is absolutely obsessed with tactical board games. It is a chess nut. Apparently quite hard to conquer as well.

IAIN MACDONALD

. . . .

My girlfriend says she gets turned off when I constantly talk to her about farming machinery. That's a shame because I don't know how else I could a tractor.

SEAN HEGARTY

. . . .

I had some sheep who I made run faster than they were used to, but it just made them all sweaty. Last time I try overflocking my seepy ewe.

LAURA MONMOTH

. . . .

Little horses are shy. Big horses are shire.

KEVIN HUDSON

. . . .

A friend of mine had a sore throat after grooming one of the ponies at the stables. He felt a little horse.

HENRY DAWE

. . . .

Question for anyone who's into fly fishing – what's the most flies you've ever caught?

SEAN PATRICK

. . . .

I've been listening to *The Archers*, but I'm not sure I'm their target audience.

PAULINE EYRE

. . . .

My ex has been trying to win me back by sending me British wildlife. I wish he'd stop badgering me.

ADELE CLIFF

. . . .

After poor ratings, the BBC's *Winterwatch* programme is to move to ITV and be rebranded as *Bitterns Got Talons*.

RICHARD PULSFORD

. . . .

The distribution of crops in the countryside is just like medicine. All controlled by Big Pharma.

PHILIP SIMON

. . . .

I'm an expert at mini golf
and that's putting it mildly.

MASAI GRAHAM

. . . .

I didn't know it was possible to follow the JCB
my ex-girlfriend stole from me, but I did it; I tractor!

KAT MOLINARI

. . . .

I watched an ITV detective show where all the actors
are shepherds, it was called *Midsomer Herders*.

CHRIS NORTON WALKER

. . . .

When I'm in the countryside I always use the
bookies, which is run by woodland creatures.
I like to hedge my bets.

COLIN LEGGO

. . . .

I got told that I was rubbish at being a shepherd,
but I'm not going to lose any sheep over it.

STEVIE VEGAS

. . . .

I've typed the coordinates into Google Maps
over 7,000 times, yet I still cannot find the
land I've just purchased at auction.
My family think I've lost the plot.

SEAN HEGARTY

. . . .

I work on a farm, but it sounds more impressive
when I say I work as a 'farm assist'.

JOSEPH MURPHY

. . . .

I've got a tractor that I only use to collect my honey.
It's just to get from hay to bee.

IAIN MACDONALD

. . . .

Just heard that my uncle had a heart attack while
hiking in Sherwood forest. Apparently he's OK,
but not yet out of the woods.

TONY COWARDS

. . . .

A chicken has been banished from a coop after
growing too large. It was ostrich-sized.

DARREN WALSH

. . . .

The host of *Countryfile* quit after reading the works of
Edgar Allan Poe – 'Quoth the Craven "Nevermore"'.

LAURA MONMOTH

. . . .

My friend Susan, who owns a dairy farm, always cures
my headaches by tickling me. So, the next time you've
got a headache just remember that farmer Sue tickles.

KEVIN HUDSON

. . . .

I split my bellbottom jeans climbing over a gate into the next field. I'm over that stile now anyway.

PAULINE EYRE

•••••••••••••••••••••

When I was trying to cross from one field to another on my ramble over the weekend, I came across the biggest stile I had ever seen in my life. I couldn't get over it.

HENRY DAWE

•••••••••••••••••••••

THE JUNGLE

I put my parents on a branch to see if it would
make them taller. It worked on my dad,
but Mummy doesn't grow on trees.

ADELE CLIFF

....

I brought a little lizard back from the jungle
and it now keeps an eye on our newborn child.
It makes a great baby monitor.

RICHARD PULSFORD

....

Guns 'n' Roses are starting a new campaign to
help people open up about athlete's foot.
It's called 'Welcome to the Fungal'.

KAT MOLINARI

....

If you're going to a jungle dinner party,
enjoy a canapé.

CHRIS NORTON WALKER

....

I met this lion who was so embarrassed because he
couldn't bring himself to eat any of the other lions.
I said, 'Oh come on, swallow your pride!'

COLIN LEGGO

....

Last night a man was hung by his own
long-snouted animal. Imagine that, being
hoisted by your own pet aardvark.

ROB THOMAS

· · · · · · · · · · · · · · · · · · · ·

Couldn't get any phone reception in the jungle
till I signed up to Tree Mobile.

STEVIE VEGAS

· · · · · · · · · · · · · · · · · · · ·

I sat in my living room in front of a roaring fire and
wondered, *Why is there a lion on fire in my house?*

JOSEPH MURPHY

· · · · · · · · · · · · · · · · · · · ·

I had an audition for the part of the bear
in *The Jungle Book*. I Baloo it.

ANDREW TYMMS

· · · · · · · · · · · · · · · · · · · ·

A pirate had his great ape and some treasure stolen
from him. He didn't care too much for the gold,
but he wanted his silverback.

IAIN MACDONALD

· · · · · · · · · · · · · · · · · · · ·

What's the difference between a hippo and a Zippo?
One's really heavy and the other one's a little lighter.

MASAI GRAHAM

· · · · · · · · · · · · · · · · · · · ·

What's the rudest animal in the jungle?
The hippo potty mouth.

TONY COWARDS

....

Just got back from the Amazon, converting the natives to Christianity. Was a right mission.

DARREN WALSH

....

I've always had a keen interest in jungles. It's a pity I can't find someone who'll show me the ropes.

SEAN HEGARTY

....

I saw a dessert made of sugar and almonds swinging through the jungle. Pretty sure it was tarzipan.

LAURA MONMOTH

....

Tarzan was really good at writing radio ads
— he was King of the Jingle.

KEVIN HUDSON

....

An updated version of Jimmy Perry's and David Croft's classic jungle sitcom would have gone down very well with computer scientists: *It Ain't Half Hot Motherboard*, starring Donald Hewlett Packard.

HENRY DAWE

....

'Work hard, play hard.'

'Yes. Is there anything you do find easy, Mr Tarzan?'

SEAN PATRICK

. . . .

'Oh my God, did you see those tree frogs?'

'No, just the two.'

PAULINE EYRE

. . . .

Tarzan met his wife in the Jane forest.

ADELE CLIFF

. . . .

There are two weird features of the national bird of the African country closest to Madagascar, which is nose and beak.

RICHARD PULSFORD

. . . .

When George of the Jungle hits his head on a tree, he gets a bit spinney.

KAT MOLINARI

. . . .

I was recently in *The X-Factor* Jungle. It's got a very delicate Chico-system.

CHRIS NORTON WALKER

. . . .

What's the main blood disease among the larger safari animals? Hippo-titus.

COLIN LEGGO

....

I now do all my banking in the jungle, although sometimes I go to the wrong branch.

STEVIE VEGAS

....

Mila Kunis stole Timon and Pumbaa's fish sauce. Pumbaa shouted, 'Ay, Kunis, my tartare!'

JOSEPH MURPHY

....

I used to be a lion tamer, but less than a month into the job they sacked me. I never felt as though I got a fair crack of the whip.

ANDREW TYMMS

....

A friend of mine told me to go and ask a gorilla what family order he belonged to. I replied, 'I don't like to pry, mate.'

IAIN MACDONALD

....

'Ahhhhhh! Ahhhhhhh! Ahhhhhhhh!' – Tarzan (at the dentist).

SEAN HEGARTY

....

Why is the Amazon so big? Jungle is massive.

MASAI GRAHAM

....

I went to a golf tournament in the jungle. It was hopeless, I couldn't see Tiger Woods for the trees.

KEVIN HUDSON

....

There are some beautiful girls to be found in the Amazon rainforest. They call them jungle belles.

HENRY DAWE

....

Someone else said there was a chameleon, but I can't see it myself.

PAULINE EYRE

....

PUBLIC TRANSPORT

There's a special docking place for ships that go by 'he' instead of 'she'. It's a public trans port.

KAT MOLINARI

....

I saw a documentary about people who have sex with their cars, looked exhausting.

ADELE CLIFF

....

My local council are so keen to get the buses to run on time that they're pulling out all the stops.

RICHARD PULSFORD

....

I tried to take the bus home yesterday, couldn't get it through the front door though.

RICHARD WOOLFORD

....

Ticket inspectors, you've got to hand it to them.

CHRIS NORTON WALKER

....

Was late to my maths exam today.
I took the rhombus.

JOSEPH MURPHY

....

What type of trousers do Uber drivers wear
while drinking coffee? Cabbie chinos.

COLIN LEGGO

. . . .

I'm going to create a village called Not-in-Service
so anyone who lives there will always be
able to get a bus home.

ROB THOMAS

. . . .

There's a new soap on TV about different
passenger vehicles. I've missed the first few
episodes, but I'll catch the omnibus.

STEVIE VEGAS

. . . .

Some pure silver took my bus fare.
It was the conductor.

IAIN MACDONALD

. . . .

Took my automobile to a mechanic who was
having a seizure, luckily it was a Kwik Fit.

LOVDEV BARPAGA

. . . .

I drove over 200 miles to a *Star Wars* convention
in a Ford seven-seater. When I got there,
I was in a Galaxy far, far away.

MASAI GRAHAM

. . . .

Best way to get on a Japanese bus quickly? Nippon.

TONY COWARDS

. . . .

I started a limo company,
but I've got nothing to chauffeur it.

LEO KEARSE

. . . .

> *Gameshow Host:* What do you use to get free entry on to a bus?

> *ME:* Pass!

> *Gameshow Host:* Correct!

SEAN HEGARTY

. . . .

If you experience pain when travelling on one of those electric-powered vehicles running on rails in the road, there's a specific medication for it: tramadol.

HENRY DAWE

. . . .

I was once on the back seat of a bus sat between the Greek god of war and Guy Garvey. I'm not sure which was which as I didn't know my Ares from my Elbow.

RICHARD PULSFORD

. . . .

I pulled out my guitar and played Elvis songs
on the way to work – I was bus king.

PAULINE EYRE

....

If ever I need cheering up, I get the bus to Keaton.

KEVIN HUDSON

....

My friend's job is motivating people to use
more swearwords. He's a cuss driver.

KAT MOLINARI

....

Found the front of a car in my allotment.
Bumper crop.

CHRIS NORTON WALKER

....

Since the day I bought a forward-facing seat
on the train, I've never looked back.

COLIN LEGGO

....

My double-decker bus helps pull up vegetables.
It's a root master.

STEVIE VEGAS

....

I failed my driving test.
The instructor went through the roof.

JOSEPH MURPHY

....

Have you heard that National Rail have got a new chief executive? It's part of a boss-replacement service.

ANDREW TYMMS

....

The bride was so angry that the back of her dress slowed her down, she wanted to take a bus down the aisle! I thought it was best if I took the train.

IAIN MACDONALD

....

In the old days they'd have someone on buses walking up and down selling tickets. Some of them were really quick – they were lightning conductors.

KEVIN HUDSON

....

This guy tried to sell me a car with a broken satnav. I had to tell him where to go.

MASAI GRAHAM

....

I always go the extra mile, which is why I have a terrible Uber rating.

TONY COWARDS

....

I was driving around looking for a doctor's surgery, but my satnav didn't have GPs.

DARREN WALSH

....

Ran for the coach today, he made me do ten laps.

LOVDEV BARPAGA

....

My blind friend just texted me to say that he was touching himself on a bus. Where does he get off?

SEAN HEGARTY

....

The man behind the Routemaster has been honoured with a bronze bus in Westminster Abbey.

HENRY DAWE

....

TRAINS

My son had a birthday cake in the shape
of a train. He tried swallowing it whole,
but I was like, 'Chew! Chew!'

PHILIP SIMON

....

I once got chatted up by an old-fashioned
train driver, it got very steamy.

ADELE CLIFF

....

Most trains in Northamptonshire
have a Kettering service.

RICHARD PULSFORD

....

I hear David Bowie really likes it when the
old train is replaced by the new train.
He loves those choo-choo changes.

RICHARD WOOLFORD

....

The Earth's most energetic pathways are found
along the most problematic train routes.
Especially de-ley lines.

PHILIP SIMON

....

I thought I saw those famous brothers that say 'to me to you' on a train once, but it must've just been the lighting. It was shuttle vision.

KAT MOLINARI

....

I saw a train covered in cheese and tomatoes – pizza express.

CHRIS NORTON WALKER

....

I've been putting off stopping a high-speed Japanese train with my teeth but I'm going to have to bite the bullet.

COLIN LEGGO

....

Just had an announcement on the train I'm on: 'Delays on all London Underground trains from approximately 1730 onwards,' and I thought, *He knows his history*.

ROB THOMAS

....

Happy birthday to the Forth Bridge. Seems to have aged better than the first, second and third bridges.

STEVIE VEGAS

....

At the train station, I disguised myself as suspicious luggage. I got carried away.

JOSEPH MURPHY

....

I used to really like travelling by train but I've since gone completely off the rails.

ANDREW TYMMS

. . . .

Did you hear about the Mexican that wanted to have sex with a train? No one knows why but he must have had a *loco* motive.

IAIN MACDONALD

. . . .

The conductor said to me, 'Ticket or pass?', I said, 'Well, in that case, I think I'll pass'.

MASAI GRAHAM

. . . .

I really love railway platforms; in fact, I get off on them.

TONY COWARDS

. . . .

I wear platform shoes, but I take them off once I'm on the train.

DARREN WALSH

. . . .

'Ladies and gentlemen, we have just realised that we have neglected to put any little tickets behind the seats to indicate where you have booked. We apologise unreservedly.'

HENRY DAWE

. . . .

I watched *The Girl On the Train* last night. To be honest, the first ten minutes were really good then she reported me to the conductor, and I got kicked off.

SEAN HEGARTY

. . . .

The Queen's personal train driver has quit after becoming a republican. He's gone off the royals.

LAURA MONMOTH

. . . .

There was a different cat on my train this morning – it was a replacement-puss service.

KEVIN HUDSON

. . . .

When you're learning to drive them, does that make you a trainee? Do they have gears, or do you use the training manual?

PAULINE EYRE

. . . .

I hired security staff for a train journey that cost one third less than normal. It was a 16–25 rail guard.

ADELE CLIFF

. . . .

So, I was telling my friend how I hate backgammon. And draughts. He said, 'Hate chess too?' I said, 'Don't even get me started on that high-speed rail project.'

RICHARD PULSFORD

. . . .

I was trainspotting with a friend when we saw a freight train carrying only Oxo cubes. My mate said, 'Oh look, it's the gravy train.' I said, 'No, just rolling stock.'

NIGEL LOVELL

....

I hear Thomas the Tank Engine likes dressing up as a lady, he's a trainsvestite.

RICHARD WOOLFORD

....

My sister always wanted to be a train operator like dad, so he taught her how to conductor self.

KAT MOLINARI

....

To supplement his income my DJ friend works for British Rail, he loves laying down some tracks.

CHRIS NORTON WALKER

....

My friend Luca once committed murder on a train. Police never did work out a Luca-motive.

COLIN LEGGO

....

Almost finished my first album about building a railroad. Just got to lay down a few more tracks.

STEVIE VEGAS

....

I've just had 40 winks on the train.
This aftershave is incredible!

JOSEPH MURPHY

....

What's a crab's favourite railway depot?
Kings Crustacean.

ANDREW TYMMS

....

I volunteered for the task of being a train, but it
seems that I bit off more than I could choo-choo.

IAIN MACDONALD

....

I saw a bigot picking out victims at a
railway station he was trans-spotting.

LOVDEV BARPAGA

....

My friend Tracy works at the train station,
or as we like to call her, Track and Trace.

MASAI GRAHAM

....

At the State Opening of Parliament in 2015,
my cousin's little boy had the honour of carrying
The Queen's train. Unfortunately, it was
20 minutes overdue.

HENRY DAWE

....

London trains were banned in 1863, which only
served to drive them underground.

TONY COWARDS

....

I asked someone from Birmingham which train
was the Slough one. Been on here bloody ages.

DARREN WALSH

....

My latest album is called *Railway*
because it's only got two tracks.

SEAN HEGARTY

....

A friend has been painting pictures of trains
all over town. They're his local motifs.

LAURA MONMOTH

....

I got myself a ticket for cheap Spanish
train travel – a *señor* rail card.

KEVIN HUDSON

....

I just prefer buses, OK? Or trams!
I just prefer them. I'm not trainsphobic!

PAULINE EYRE

....

CURRENT
AFFAIRS

POLITICS

Boris Johnson may have been pro-Brexit,
but he's obsessed with French cheese and
eats it regularly. It's a daily brie thing.

PAULINE EYRE

....

Whenever I watch *Prime Minister's Questions*
there's a man running around naked,
I think it's the streaker of the house.

ADELE CLIFF

....

Someone just threw a comic at President Trump.
I think it was a Walt Disney one. Well, whoever
it was, made Donald duck.

RICHARD PULSFORD

....

What do Boris Johnson and Jennifer Arcuri sing
at Christmas? 'Oh Come, All Ye Unfaithful'.

RICHARD WOOLFORD

....

If you want to understand the politics of the
Middle East, factions speak louder than Kurds.

PHILIP SIMON

....

What's a brand of cider but also a strain of
marijuana for Tories? Thatcher's Haze.

KAT MOLINARI

....

Which politician's wife loves C. S. Lewis books?
Mel-Narnia Trump.

CHRIS NORTON WALKER

....

It's taken me ages to write a pun about how
I fancy Keir Starmer, Ed Miliband and Gordon Brown.
It's a labour of love.

COLIN LEGGO

....

When you vote, read the signs carefully
because there's a big difference between
a ballot box and a bollox bat.

ROB THOMAS

....

Corbyn wanted us to vote for the three of
diamonds, but Johnson insisted on the three of
spades. That's why we had a snap election.

STEVIE VEGAS

....

Why do libertarians only have flings? Because they
find serious relationships too taxing.

JOSEPH MURPHY

....

Phwoar, y'see that Katie Hopkins?
She's a bit of alt-right.

IAIN MACDONALD

. . . .

Harry wouldn't visit the ghetto streets
of Birmingham but the lady would.

LOVDEV BARPAGA

. . . .

Which former deputy prime minister is most
likely to steal a prosthetic limb? Nick Clegg.

MASAI GRAHAM

. . . .

People who show me how to vote
make me a little cross.

TONY COWARDS

. . . .

When Boris Johnson was mayor of London,
he didn't start work till the evening. That's why
some people still think he's a night mayor.

KEVIN HUDSON

. . . .

My wife went into labour last week and
I haven't seen her since. I wonder if
Keir Starmer's took her hostage?!

SEAN HEGARTY

. . . .

Told a guy that he looked like Che Guevara.
He told me I looked like Che Guevara. Two Che.

DARREN WALSH

. . . .

'Hello, I'm Keir ... St ... St ... St ... Stammer.'

EL BALDINHO

. . . .

Toby Young has claimed that the Dominic Cummings
scandal is a non-story, which is odd as he's the first
person I think of when I hear 'nonce Tory'.

PAUL SAVAGE

. . . .

Angela Merkel is in a very strong position to steal
a march on Germany's neighbouring countries.
With her superior oratory skills, brilliant negotiation
and robust foreign policy, she can strike a sword into
the heart of France and another sword into the heart
of Austria. Ah, good old Angela: Madame Two Swords.

HENRY DAWE

. . . .

2021 started out just impeachy.

PAULINE EYRE

. . . .

What do Boris Johnson and Jennifer Arcuri hang
on their Christmas tree? Affairy lights.

RICHARD WOOLFORD

. . . .

I saw a French man and a German man
urinating in the street, they were members
of the Europe Peeing Union.

ADELE CLIFF

. . . .

It's unlikely President Trump has slept with any
porn stars – they've usually had breast implants
and we all know he hates fake nudes.

RICHARD PULSFORD

. . . .

My partner cheated on me with an MP,
they were caught shagging in a river.
He's really into his current affairs.

KAT MOLINARI

. . . .

The House of Commons is like bad plastic surgery –
eyes to the right, nose to the left.

CHRIS NORTON WALKER

. . . .

I met the German Chancellor that's made
out of triangles: Angular Merkel.

COLIN LEGGO

. . . .

Who benefits from a hung Parliament?
Mrs Parliament.

JOSEPH MURPHY

. . . .

Relatives of those guillotined in the French Revolution are asking for an official pardon so they can finally hold their heads up high.

ROB THOMAS

....

I used to clean soldiers' housing using formaldehyde, assisted by the 42nd President of the USA. I was a barrack embalmer ... with Bill Clinton.

STEVIE VEGAS

....

Where does the prime minister shop for his groceries? Borissons.

ANDREW TYMMS

....

The former Ugandan president loved paperwork. It was Idi Admin.

IAIN MACDONALD

....

If Boris and his dad ease the Lockdown regulations, that would make Johnson and Johnson's 'No more tiers'.

MASAI GRAHAM

....

If you're ever drinking with Vladimir Putin don't ask him, 'What's your poison?'

TONY COWARDS

....

This bloke told me he needed more time to
decide whether he was a communist or not.
I think he was Stalin.

DARREN WALSH

....

I was in Parliament last week and every time I kept
trying to discuss why I think homeless people should
receive free accommodation, John Bercow kept
shouting, 'Order! Order!' To be fair though,
15 minutes had passed and quite a long queue
had formed at the tuck shop.

SEAN HEGARTY

....

People say there are no political messages in
The Lord of the Rings, but they forget about
Gandalf the White-Ring Populist.

LAURA MONMOTH

....

When middle-class people say their children
are going hungry during school holidays, they
just mean there's a family trip to Budapest.

KEVIN HUDSON

....

We must treat COVID-19 like ska,
in order to avoid a third wave.

PAUL SAVAGE

....

Seen accusations that the Black Lives Matter
protestors are being paid to destroy statues.
That's not what they meant when they said
they're pulling down six figures.

PAUL SAVAGE

. . . .

The MP for North West Leicestershire had a reputation
of being something of a lothario. When asked by a
journalist for an update on current affairs in the town,
he didn't know where to begin.

HENRY DAWE

. . . .

In January we saw un-presidented
scenes at the Capitol.

PAULINE EYRE

. . . .

I still can't believe people think the Iraq War
wasn't about oil; their arguments scrape
the bottom of the barrel.

JENAN YOUNIS

. . . .

THE ROYAL FAMILY

What king had his own chocolate factory?
William the Wonkerer.

RICHARD WOOLFORD

....

All of the Queen's attendants have to use curtsey cars.

RICHARD PULSFORD

....

I hear Queen Elizabeth I used to rub her collar up
and down on her groin, she was really into ruff sex.

RICHARD WOOLFORD

....

The official job title of a Kate Middleton
impersonator is a 'Dupli-Kate'.

KAT MOLINARI

....

The Queen was actually a brilliant gas fitter,
CORGI registered.

CHRIS NORTON WALKER

....

Why did Henry VIII get his wife glasses?
To help Jane see more.

COLIN LEGGO

....

If the Queen hands you apples remember
your first priority – decorum.

ROB THOMAS

....

I think our next monarch should be exactly
12 inches tall. They'd be a perfect ruler.

STEVIE VEGAS

....

I have just quit my job as Prince Harry's assistant.
I realised that, no matter how long or hard I worked,
I would never become Prince Harry.

JOSEPH MURPHY

....

When Henry VIII was married to his first wife,
he was obsessed with sports. Polo, football,
boxing. Oh yeah, Anne Boleyn.

IAIN MACDONALD

....

The Queen shouted at a couple of pigeons
and they both died. Talk about killing
two birds with one's tone.

MASAI GRAHAM

....

Say what you like about the Queen's judgement
but she's always on the money.

TONY COWARDS

....

When the Duchess of Cambridge went into labour, Prince William's heir started falling out.

DARREN WALSH

. . . .

Prince Andrew's a liar! I caught him playing bingo last week, he was sweating on one number.

SEAN HEGARTY

. . . .

Meghan Markle thought she was going on a shopping trip after her wedding – Harry said he was going to drive her down the Mall.

EL BALDINHO

. . . .

You never see Victorian postboxes anymore. We're starting to VR away from them.

LAURA MONMOTH

. . . .

Some say the government are using pubs reopening at six o'clock to distract the news from Prince Andrew. No idea where they got the idea of entering something way before it's usually legal.

PAUL SAVAGE

. . . .

I was, at one point, 123rd in line for the throne. Wish they had more toilets at Glastonbury.

NIGEL LOVELL

. . . .

The other day I walked past Clarence House
and spotted Prince Charles in his office, poring
over some documents. Ah, poor Prince Charles
– he never reigns, but he pores.

HENRY DAWE

· · · · · · · · · · · · · · · · · · · ·

I'm not saying the Queen has been spreading
COVID-19, but they're monitoring her
Elizabeth R number.

PAULINE EYRE

· · · · · · · · · · · · · · · · · · · ·

The Queen's put on a few pounds.

FRIZ FRIZZLE

· · · · · · · · · · · · · · · · · · · ·

Why's Henry's wife covered in tooth marks?
Because he's Tudor.

ADELE CLIFF

· · · · · · · · · · · · · · · · · · · ·

MI5 have foiled a plot designed to assassinate
Prince Charles in Westminster Abbey
using a service to heir missile.

RICHARD PULSFORD

· · · · · · · · · · · · · · · · · · · ·

Prince Charles showing house viewers his wife's toilet:
... And this is where she likes to 'Parker Bowles'.

KAT MOLINARI

· · · · · · · · · · · · · · · · · · · ·

I can tell you Prince Andrew's favourite restaurants?
Sure, no sweat.

CHRIS NORTON WALKER

....

Apparently, the royal photocopier won't produce
images of Harry, but it prints William.

COLIN LEGGO

....

I'd love to see a fight between Prince William,
will.i.am, Will Smith and Will Ferrell — it'd be a
real battle of the various celebrities.

ROB THOMAS

....

If I can manage to sell hot beverages to Prince Charles,
do you think I could live off the royal teas?

STEVIE VEGAS

....

I told an audience to give me any subject and I'll
make a pun out of it. They shouted, 'The Queen'
and I replied, 'The Queen isn't a subject.'

JOSEPH MURPHY

....

The Queen has a pig as her servant.
It's at her bacon call.

IAIN MACDONALD

....

The Queen can hit a tennis ball farther than any member of the royal family. That's why she's our longest serving monarch.

MASAI GRAHAM

. . . .

The Queen is so old that nowadays she can only get around with the aid of a nobility scooter.

TONY COWARDS

. . . .

Princess Diana's family wanted everyone at her funeral to wear 'smart casual'. Bloody Marxist Spencers.

DARREN WALSH

. . . .

I charged the Queen £100 once after going to the bathroom in Windsor Castle. I had a royal flush.

SEAN HEGARTY

. . . .

Charles has been known to send other members of the royal family pictures from his treks around the UK but most people prefer his prints of Wales.

GRAHAM MUSK

. . . .

A queen, a bishop and a castle walked into a bar. The barman looked at the castle and said, 'Sorry, I can't serve him, he can't walk straight.'

LAURA MONMOTH

. . . .

I was at school with Charles the First. We called him that because he won all the races on sports day.

KEVIN HUDSON

....

My girlfriend wants me to treat her like a princess, so I've got the media to stir up racial hatred against her.

PAUL SAVAGE

....

'Admit it, Charles,' said The Queen, 'you only bought me that CD of *The Goon Show* so that you could borrow it and learn all the silly voices to impress your friends at parties. It's always the same with you, Charles – one minute you're all serious about being groomed as my successor, and the next you're acting the fool. It's a classic case of heir today, goon tomorrow.'

HENRY DAWE

....

She has a special room for her make-up
– it's her Elizabeth R-den

PAULINE EYRE

....

GLOBAL WARMING

To protest global warming Germans are pouring wine into the oceans, so now sea levels are Reisling.

PHILIP SIMON

. . . .

My fruit shop owner has recently been sourcing all his food locally and has been cutting down on his emissions. He is now my green grocer.

STEVIE VEGAS

. . . .

As the Arctic warms up we must make decisions on what to do about the polar bears now. These things can't just be de-furred.

RICHARD PULSFORD

. . . .

I saw the real Spider-Man out of costume at an environmental convention and he held his hand up to say hello. It was a Pete-wave.

KAT MOLINARI

. . . .

Ditched my mates to go diving at the Great Barrier Reef. You know what they say, keep your friends close but your anemones closer.

CHRIS NORTON WALKER

. . . .

Which serial killer operates 20–30km above
the earth? The Ozone Slayer.

ADELE CLIFF

....

My house made out of warm bread fell
into the sea. Toastal erosion.

COLIN LEGGO

....

I told a flat-earther to walk around the Earth's
equator. He eventually came around.

JOSEPH MURPHY

....

My next-door neighbour insists on wearing
thick tights, even in hot weather.
He's a climate change denier.

ANDREW TYMMS

....

I moved out of the biggest city in Austria to the
second-biggest city because of pollution.
Turns out that the Graz is greener.

IAIN MACDONALD

....

Politicians keep saying nuclear power is the
way to save the planet; I just think they're
fission around for easy answers.

JENAN YOUNIS

....

Did you hear about the couple who moved into an orchard? They lived appley ever after.

ANDREW TYMMS

· · · · · · · · · · · · · · · · · · · ·

I painted my home a mixture of yellow and blue. I gave it the greenhouse effect.

MASAI GRAHAM

· · · · · · · · · · · · · · · · · · · ·

I was once asked to judge a competition for sustainable energy, I was on the solar panel.

TONY COWARDS

· · · · · · · · · · · · · · · · · · · ·

It wasn't till Linda married Paul McCartney that I knew who she was. I hadn't heard of herbivore.

DARREN WALSH

· · · · · · · · · · · · · · · · · · · ·

My local hat manufacturer is contributing to global warming. Every time I go in, I witness the felting of a nice cap.

LAURA MONMOTH

· · · · · · · · · · · · · · · · · · · ·

At a recent global warming rally, Greta Thunberg said that the planet was struggling due to the bad atmosphere, which made me feel really guilty as myself and my wife got into an argument earlier that day.

SEAN HEGARTY

· · · · · · · · · · · · · · · · · · · ·

Climate change deniers are fossil fools.

PAULINE EYRE

....

Two women who have just been pensioned off have made it their mission to release high levels of carbon dioxide into the atmosphere. They're also planning to meet up every day for coffee. So, they'll be spending all their retirement gassing.

HENRY DAWE

....

I do worry about global warming melting the Antarctic glaciers, but that really is just the tip of the iceberg.

JENAN YOUNIS

....

Kermit the Frog is environmentally conscious but like a lot of us, sometimes he struggles to put it into practice. It's not easy being green.

ANDREW TYMMS

....

I saw the famous environmental campaigner Ms Thunberg with her boyfriend today. I thought, *Oh, Greta room!*

COLIN LEGGO

....

Vin Diesel's annoyed with the UK government.
He's got till 2040 to change his name to Vin Electric.

KEVIN HUDSON

....

What fruit has razor-sharp teeth? A pear-hana.

ANDREW TYMMS

....

My thoughts on how to conserve the Arctic and
Antarctic divide men's opinions. I polarise chaps.

ADELE CLIFF

....

Wind turbine impressions? Well, I'm a massive fan.

RICHARD PULSFORD

....

This summer, there shall be no more colonics for
sex workers due to the hoes pipe ban.

CHRIS NORTON WALKER

....

In order to reduce my carbon footprint, I have
decided not to wear my carbon shoes anymore.

STEVIE VEGAS

....

If the changes of weather were on
top of a mountain, I'd climate.

IAIN MACDONALD

....

I've been to the year 2050
Not much has changed but they live underwater
And your great, great, great granddaughter
Is pretty annoyed, you didn't cut carbon emissions
(Carbon emissions)

JOSEPH MURPHY

....

I've written a joke about the *Titanic*.
It's a one-liner in two parts.

MASAI GRAHAM

....

My girlfriend said that the red doorbell I bought
her isn't very environmentally friendly.
I might buy 'er da grey doorbell.

DARREN WALSH

....

My friend's blaming global warming on the glaciers
but if you ask me, I think the owners of Manchester
United have nothing to do with it.

SEAN HEGARTY

....

When you talk about environmentalists, do their
ears burn? That would be lobal warming.

EL BALDINHO

....

Globally, water levels are rising
but in Germany, wine levels are Riesling.

KEVIN HUDSON

. . . .

If global warming continues at this rate, the
beleaguered environment minister is going
to need all the fans he can get.

HENRY DAWE

. . . .

FOOD AND DRINK

FRUIT

Trying to win lots of fruit on eBay.
My currant bid is £0.50.

STEVIE VEGAS

....

The best fruit films I've seen are *Hot Tub Lime Machine*,
Planet of the Grapes and *Cherry Maguire*.

ADELE CLIFF

....

Pot Noodle contains a subliminal message
to reassure you that it's not poodle.

ROB THOMAS

....

I grew up in Saudi Arabia because my dad had
a job there working with oil. He was a chef.

ZAHRA BARRI

....

What's the number one Japanese citrus fruit sport?
Satsumo wrestling.

RICHARD WOOLFORD

....

The most Zen-like of all fruits is, of course, the lychi.

PHILIP SIMON

....

Brexit has affected the importing of
Mediterranean fruit such as figs and prunes.
It's also brought an end to freedom of movement.

RICHARD PULSFORD

· · · · · · · · · · · · · · · · · · · ·

Tina Turner likes her oranges skinless
because it's better than all the zest.

KAT MOLINARI

· · · · · · · · · · · · · · · · · · · ·

Best fruit-based military leader? Che Guava.

CHRIS NORTON WALKER

· · · · · · · · · · · · · · · · · · · ·

Last night I saw a man at the bar chatting up
a woman while covered in mashed-up fruit,
I thought, *What a smoothie!*

TONY COWARDS

· · · · · · · · · · · · · · · · · · · ·

They sent palm tree fruit into space.
The world's first coconaut.

JOSEPH MURPHY

· · · · · · · · · · · · · · · · · · · ·

An eighties girl band once chased me while throwing
knives and the only thing I had to shield myself with
was a bunch of fruit. It was banana armour.

KAT MOLINARI

· · · · · · · · · · · · · · · · · · · ·

The insides of apples are sexy aren't they? Core!

COLIN LEGGO

....

This little orange fruit was trying to force the other fruit out of the fruit bowl by pushing and slapping them. It was a satsumo.

IAIN MACDONALD

....

My dad was a Jamaican greengrocer.
He always had lots of melon in.

MASAI GRAHAM

....

My ex-wife took me to court about a dispute over who owned our apple pies. She got custardy.

DARREN WALSH

....

What's the best way to start a joke about fruit?
Mangoes into a bar ...

SEAN HEGARTY

....

My Moroccan cookery tour is proving very popular.
I've just added a few more dates.

EL BALDINHO

....

I like a really big Japanese fruit — a satsumo.

KEVIN HUDSON

....

Eton Mess: dormitory.

HENRY DAWE

....

**'How you like DEM apples?' (Me on my first day
as tour guide at the apple museum.)**

SEAN PATRICK

....

**I was making my own citrus-flavoured smoothie but
I forgot to put the lid on the food processor and got
totally splattered. I looked like a right lemon.**

JENAN YOUNIS

....

**I got in a sticky situation at the World Strawberry
Yogurt Boxing Championships when someone
backed me into a fruit corner.**

ADELE CLIFF

....

**People ask me why I only eat dried fruit
but all I'll say is, I have my raisins.**

RICHARD PULSFORD

....

**I crushed dried grapes into some coins before
donating them to my local shelter. Hopefully no
one will complain because, at the end of the day,
it's raisin money for charity.**

SEAN HEGARTY

....

A magician was crushing basil and
pine nuts when suddenly, 'Hey pesto!'

ROB THOMAS

....

I didn't know where to keep all these fruit-based
jokes, till a friend suggested a pun net?

PHILIP SIMON

....

Pineapple rings, I didn't answer though.

RICHARD WOOLFORD

....

I was punched for singing a fruit version of
'Common People', in fact I was beaten to a pulp.

CHRIS NORTON WALKER

....

I took part in a fruit-eating contest in Rio de Janeiro.
I managed all the apples but I couldn't cope a banana.

COLIN LEGGO

....

Not sure I could choose just one fruit as my favourite.
Would anyone mind if I picked a pear?

STEVIE VEGAS

....

I eat more bananas than monkeys. I've eaten over
10,000 bananas and not a single monkey.

JOSEPH MURPHY

....

Yorkshire Police went to arrest this little
orange fruit. It refused to kumquat-ly.

IAIN MACDONALD

. . . .

Bananas. One of your Fyffe a day.

MASAI GRAHAM

. . . .

Been asked to do some gigs for a dried-fruit company,
just waiting for them to get back to me with some dates.

TONY COWARDS

. . . .

My currant girlfriend just dumped me.
I guess everything happens for a raisin.

DARREN WALSH

. . . .

I love fusion food; my favourite is Scottish-Egyptian
cooked by Gordon Rameses.

EL BALDINHO

. . . .

When he failed to get a part in *The Grapes of Wrath*,
Jack Lemmon was pretty sour.

HENRY DAWE

. . . .

How do you make a mango? Ask him to marry you.

PAULINE EYRE

. . . .

ALCOHOL

I'm a bit worried I might have contracted
malaria at a cocktail bar last night.
I came home covered in mojito bites.

ADELE CLIFF

....

Me and my friend were 16 the first time
I tried tequila, but that's enough about
my attempted murders.

ADELE CLIFF

....

I was consoling my friend in the pub, whose
girlfriend had told him he was fat. I said,
'Don't worry about that. Your round, mate.'

RICHARD PULSFORD

....

What happens when the Spice Girls drink too much?
They're sick-a-sick-ah.

RICHARD WOOLFORD

....

Satan has a new drinking game that involves
mixing eggs, sugar and brandy. Seems vile,
but he's just playing devil's Advocate.

PHILIP SIMON

....

I trained my dog to fetch me my bottle of gin so
that I didn't have to get up. He's my spirit animal.

KAT MOLINARI

....

Walked into a Nazi pub where
I found Schindlers pissed.

CHRIS NORTON WALKER

....

How does Bradley Walsh like his Liquor?
With a Chaser.

CHRIS NORTON WALKER

....

I love that soap about a group of Londoners
who brew beer up their bums – *Yeast-Enders*.

COLIN LEGGO

....

Chap at my party asked if we had any mulled wine.
I told him to give me a few minutes to think
about it, and then gave him some wine.

ROB THOMAS

....

Whenever I go to the pub with my mum's
crochet class, they never offer to buy me a
drink. They're a tight knit community!

ANDREW TYMMS

....

Got a job removing vodka directly from the heart.
I'm a Bacardiologist.

STEVIE VEGAS

....

My dog has a bit of a drink problem.
He's a borderline alcohollie.

ANDREW TYMMS

....

Why do all wine waiters stink? Cos they're sommelier.

IAIN MACDONALD

....

A German began choking on his beer. I saved
them using the Heineken manoeuvre.

LOVDEV BARPAGA

....

I grew up around a family of alcoholics.
I blame my foster parents.

MASAI GRAHAM

....

My job at the brewery was to check the alcoholic
content on the beer bottles, I was the proof reader.

TONY COWARDS

....

'Man walks into a tavern— Oh, you won't get it!
It's an inn joke.'

DARREN WALSH

....

I'm 60 days clean now. It's been hard showering
so much but at least I had large quantities
of alcohol to help me through it.

JOSEPH MURPHY

....

Just got home from watching the charity cricket game
for alcoholics. England beat Ireland by three WKDs.

SEAN HEGARTY

....

I asked the lady at the off-licence how strong the
vodka was and she said, 'That one's 40 per cent proof,'
and then shouted, 'BUT THAT ONE IS 50 PER CENT
PROOF!' It was obviously more alcohol by volume.

EL BALDINHO

....

Toasting. It's enough to raise anyone's spirits.

GRAHAM MUSK

....

I mixed rum, coconut cream and pineapple juice
together when a black hole suddenly appeared
in my glass. It was a large piña collider.

LAURA MONMOTH

....

The croupier offered me a double scotch,
but I thought it was two whisky.

KEVIN HUDSON

....

Sure, Prosecco is pretentious
but Poetryco is much worse.

PAUL SAVAGE

....

I've joined the AAAA. It's for people
who are being driven to drink.

HENRY DAWE

....

My sister and I have been making home brew for
spies. She tasted our product first. She took one sip
and had insider cider inside 'er.

PAULINE EYRE

....

My friend runs a multicultural-themed bar
– they only serve cosmopolitans.

JENAN YOUNIS

....

My dad's home brew used to make us all ill.
What was wrong with it? Well, it wasn't actually clear.

RICHARD PULSFORD

....

Got into a fight with the guys from *Hamilton*,
who were insisting I couldn't have any more
alcohol in tiny glasses. I insisted that,
'I am not throwing away my shot.'

STEVIE VEGAS

....

During a power cut in the pub I had to guess the spirit
I was drinking, which was a shot in the dark.

RICHARD WOOLFORD

．．．．．．．．．．．．．．．．．．．

There's a new ale called Prototype. It's a draft beer.

PHILIP SIMON

．．．．．．．．．．．．．．．．．．．

I once worked in a recycling warehouse for
Mexican beer bottles. It was Sol destroying.

KAT MOLINARI

．．．．．．．．．．．．．．．．．．．

Went to prison in Mexico where the bars tasted of
salt, lemon and regret. It was a tequila slammer.

CHRIS NORTON WALKER

．．．．．．．．．．．．．．．．．．．

I hear that they're now only selling pale ales in
tablet form. That's a bitter pill to swallow.

COLIN LEGGO

．．．．．．．．．．．．．．．．．．．

Me and my mates did some research into the
effects of alcohol. The results were staggering.

ROB THOMAS

．．．．．．．．．．．．．．．．．．．

A guy in a pub called me cheap.
I was so shocked I almost spit out his drink.

JOSEPH MURPHY

．．．．．．．．．．．．．．．．．．．

Have you heard about the injured rabbit beer?
Barely Hops.

IAIN MACDONALD

....

I passed my space-cadet training programme while I
was drunk, which is great 'cause I'm really into Stella.

LOVDEV BARPAGA

....

My mate signed us both up to the Army.
All I said was, 'Let's get tanked up!'

MASAI GRAHAM

....

JK Rowling originally wrote a story about a wizard
who did alcohol-based magic called Beetrix Potter.

TONY COWARDS

....

My workmates think I'm an alcoholic.
I'm wasted in this job.

DARREN WALSH

....

I went into the pub and the barman said,
'Hi, how can I help you?' I asked, 'Do you have
draught?' He replied, 'Yes, sorry about that.
We have to keep the back doors open
because we're expecting a delivery!'

SEAN HEGARTY

....

A lot of people like drinking Pimm's at the Wimbledon Men's Final but I prefer Mixed Doubles.

EL BALDINHO

....

I find the best cure for a hangover is a Devon cream tea. It's beer today, scone tomorrow.

EL BALDINHO

....

I gave up my career as a shady pub landlord as I didn't want to spend my life behind bars.

GRAHAM MUSK

....

The brewery wants to take my pub away, but I refuse to give Inns.

LOVDEV BARPAGA

....

I like my *QI* presenters to be half human and half lemonade. My favourite is Shandi Toksvig.

LAURA MONMOTH

....

I've joined a club for people who drink beer very fast. It's called Speed CAMRA.

KEVIN HUDSON

....

Babycham: pretending to be pregnant.

HENRY DAWE

....

I had some of that pear cider while I was in labour – the midwife said I was perry-natal.

PAULINE EYRE

. . . .

I've heard of yards of ale, but can you have a metre of vodka? I know it sounds like a long shot.

FRIZ FRIZZLE

. . . .

VEGETABLES

I caught my ex watching some very niche, Green Giant-related videos online. Sweet-porn on the knob.

ADELE CLIFF

....

My German vegan friend has overtrousers made from vegetables. She calls them her *ober* jeans.

RICHARD PULSFORD

....

Onion rings, I didn't answer though.

RICHARD WOOLFORD

....

I made a vegetarian dish in the shape of that kid from *Home Alone*. Macaulay flower cheese.

KAT MOLINARI

....

Grape producer Carly Simon sings to her plants – 'You're so vine, I bet you think this wine about you ... '

CHRIS NORTON WALKER

....

What did the potato say when no one laughed at his joke? I'll get my jacket.

SEAN HEGARTY

....

The chef at my local restaurant has employed the
Grim Reaper to finely cut his vegetables.
He's dicing with death!

COLIN LEGGO

. . . .

Currently in charge of frozen vegetables and
managing the long lines of customers at Iceland.
I'm minding my peas and queues.

STEVIE VEGAS

. . . .

I tried looking into the Large Hadron Colander,
but I strained my eyes.

JOSEPH MURPHY

. . . .

My pet rodent just loves chickpeas.
He's a hoummouster.

ANDREW TYMMS

. . . .

This guy was telling me how to make guacamole
but I insisted that cucumber was the main
ingredient. I was playing devil's avocado.

IAIN MACDONALD

. . . .

I quit my job selling vegetables over my pay.
It was a celery dispute.

MASAI GRAHAM

. . . .

This morning my lip tasted of shredded
cabbage, carrot and mayonnaise; I think
I may be getting a coleslaw.

TONY COWARDS

....

Some vegetables are like pretentious puns – arty jokes.

ROB THOMAS

....

Sick of the bad treatment at the local root vegetable
farm, the workers have decided to onionise.

LAURA MONMOTH

....

I made a sofa and two armchairs out of some spuds.
They were three-piece suite potatoes.

KEVIN HUDSON

....

What chat-up line would a farmer use?
I'm zucchini on you.

JENAN YOUNIS

....

All the vegetables in the shop got together to
overthrow the system. The red onions started it.

PAULINE EYRE

....

Coriander, when mixed with carrot, is simply soup herb.

FRIZ FRIZZLE

....

Who are the only vegetables to have won the
Wimbledon Men's Singles Championships?
Björn Borg and Stefan Edberg, both Swedes.

HENRY DAWE

. . . .

As a vegan I think people who sell meat are
disgusting, but apparently people who
sell fruit and veg are grocer.

ADELE CLIFF

. . . .

I've recently been diagnosed with Asperger's but
I also have dyslexia, so it could be asparagus.

RICHARD PULSFORD

. . . .

I like to mash up chickpeas and dip my
genitals in it, I'm a houmousexual.

RICHARD WOOLFORD

. . . .

I dumped my ex-boyfriend for not washing
his willy often enough. If his penis were
an emoji, it'd be a smegplant.

KAT MOLINARI

. . . .

I've just written a series of books about onions.
Read them and weep!

COLIN LEGGO

. . . .

A wise greengrocer once said, 'Beetroot to yourself.'

CHRIS NORTON WALKER

....

Every time I eat beetroot, a little part of me dyes.

DARREN WALSH

....

Thinking of setting up a vegetarian business.
Would anyone like to become a steakholder?

STEVIE VEGAS

....

Why are seasoned comedians so sad?
Because tragedy is comedy plus thyme.

JOSEPH MURPHY

....

What's the first thing you should do if you see a
vegetarian collapsed in the street? Check for a pulse.

ANDREW TYMMS

....

Have you heard about the sad greengrocer with a
fetish for his produce? He was feeling melon coyly.

IAIN MACDONALD

....

My mother can't stop talking about her
famous spinach curry — the saga continues.

LOVDEV BARPAGA

....

Why did the Dalai Lama order a petit pois omelette?
He wanted peas *en oeuf*.

MASAI GRAHAM

....

Who called it a 'vasectomy' and not a 'parsnip'?

TONY COWARDS

....

It's nice being a giant, but I think I've
got an obsessed fan. She's beanstalking me.

DARREN WALSH

....

Why does every greengrocer stock up on buckets?
Because they keep getting leeks.

SEAN HEGARTY

....

I buy my baking products from the sheepdog
at the windmill. I love his collie flour.

KEVIN HUDSON

....

The other day I saw a man chuck a vegetable into the
library. I thought, *Now, that's a turnip for the books*.

HENRY DAWE

....

My mum left all her money to her
vegetables – those peas are minted!

PAULINE EYRE

....

CHOCOLATE

I bought my wife the new fragrance
CHOCOLAT by Cocoa Channel.

PHILIP SIMON

....

Chocoholics looking for love should try Tinder Bueno,
it's the quickest way to get in someone's snickers.

ADELE CLIFF

....

'Life is like a box of chocolates, made of leather
and zipped around your head' – *Forrest Gimp.*

RICHARD PULSFORD

....

What's Donald Trump's favourite
Quality Street flavour? Covefefe cream.

RICHARD WOOLFORD

....

I got a lift with an ambassador who was
spoiling us with his Ferrari Rocher.

PHILIP SIMON

....

What are pilots' favourite chocolate bars? Aeros.

JENAN YOUNIS

....

Washed my favourite jumper with a chocolate in the pocket, it came out covered in Lindt.

CHRIS NORTON WALKER

....

I was greeted by three police officers made out of bubbly chocolate bars, 'Areo, Areo, Areo!'

COLIN LEGGO

....

Nestlé are recalling their KitKat Chunky bars. A spokesperson said, 'Gosh, yes, I haven't had one of them in ages!'

ROB THOMAS

....

I was a very successful model for Cadbury's. People were always asking me to give them a Twirl.

STEVIE VEGAS

....

Start every morning with Aerobix. An Aero bar ground over Weetabix.

JOSEPH MURPHY

....

I had one of those great moments when you buy an item from a vending machine and two come out. It gave me an extra Boost.

LAURA MONMOTH

....

Last year, Lionel Richie bought me an Easter egg.
I cracked it open excitedly to find it empty inside.
I stared at him in complete disbelief, but he
simply shrugged and said, 'Hollow – is it
treats you're looking for?'

ANDREW TYMMS

. . . .

In my opinion, adding chocolate to coffee
just makes a mochary out of it.

IAIN MACDONALD

. . . .

My Jamaican nan wants to know why I love
chocolate spread so much but me Nutella.

MASAI GRAHAM

. . . .

What was the ancient Egyptians' favourite
chocolate bar? The Phaero.

TONY COWARDS

. . . .

What good is making a website about stranger danger
if there's a pop-up saying 'accept cookies'?

DARREN WALSH

. . . .

When's the best time to eat chocolate
at Christmas? After eight.

SEAN HEGARTY

. . . .

I bought one of those self-assembly chocolate bars
that you build into an animal. A KitCat.

KEVIN HUDSON

....

I found the chocolatier busy in his shop.
A Snickers had just toppled off the display,
so he was propping up the bar.

HENRY DAWE

....

My girlfriend likes to tie me to the bed and cover me
in caramel and chocolate. She's a dominatwix.

NIGEL LOVELL

....

Cadbury's are doing a special cockney range.
Have you tried the Trouble & Strife?

PAULINE EYRE

....

My mum insists on still calling them Marathon bars
when they haven't been called that since the eighties
– she's really got her Snickers in a twist about it.

PAULINE EYRE

....

'I've been eating lots of supermarket food,'
I said, and my friend replied, 'Waitrose?'
I said, 'Yes' dramatically.

CHRIS NORTON WALKER

....

You can get white hot chocolate now? I just don't understand why anybody would want it that hot.

KAT MOLINARI

· · · · · · · · · · · · · · · · · · ·

I keep white chocolate down my top.
The milky bras are on me!

ADELE CLIFF

· · · · · · · · · · · · · · · · · · ·

David Bowie's favourite chocolates were Revel Revel.

RICHARD PULSFORD

· · · · · · · · · · · · · · · · · · ·

Having taken over the chocolate factory Charlie struggled to pay back his debt to Willy Wonga.

PHILIP SIMON

· · · · · · · · · · · · · · · · · · ·

For every person I recruit into my workplace,
I get a giant Toblerone. It's a pyramid scheme.

KAT MOLINARI

· · · · · · · · · · · · · · · · · · ·

I saw a philosopher stood up to his knees in chocolate cake. He was deep in torte.

COLIN LEGGO

· · · · · · · · · · · · · · · · · · ·

To celebrate Hershey adopting neutral pronouns,
they're giving out free ThemThey Bars.

ROB THOMAS

· · · · · · · · · · · · · · · · · · ·

What's the most musical chocolate? Tuba Smarties.

RICHARD WOOLFORD

. . . .

I get very tetchy just before I eat my favourite chocolate sweets. I think it's just pre-Minstrel tension.

STEVIE VEGAS

. . . .

I opened my cabinet and found a three-year-old chocolate bar. There's life on Mars.

JOSEPH MURPHY

. . . .

I have invented a new device for removing the little hairs from chocolate bunnies. It's a Lindt roller.

ANDREW TYMMS

. . . .

Where did Willy Wonka hide his cocaine when the police came calling? In his charlie bucket.

IAIN MACDONALD

. . . .

I ate my Christmas chocolates so fast, we called them Ferrari Rocher.

PAULINE EYRE

. . . .

Arranged marriage proposals are like a box of chocolates, you never know what you're going to get.

LOVDEV BARPAGA

. . . .

Earlier this year, I hacked the computers at my local A&E, specifically in the section caring for people who are having allergic reactions to eating peanut butter candies. You know the ones I mean, the Resus PCs.

LAURA MONMOTH

....

What was Supernanny's favourite chocolate bar? A Time Out.

MASAI GRAHAM

....

In Roman times there were nine separate bars of chocolate in a Twix.

TONY COWARDS

....

Got woken up by a rowdy gang drinking hot milky drinks with traffic cones on their heads. Bloody alchohorlicks.

DARREN WALSH

....

What do you do if your girlfriend asks who ate all the chocolate spread? Nutella.

SEAN HEGARTY

....

My girlfriend Clare used to work at Cadbury's. That's why I call her Chocolatey Clare.

KEVIN HUDSON

....

Did you know there's a group of people who worship chocolate biscuits? Yeah, it's a breakaway religion. I say religion, it's more of a club.

NIGEL LOVELL

....

Sign on the front of Cadbury's Headquarters:
THIS SITE USES COOKIES.

HENRY DAWE

....

My chocolate company is losing money.
I won't shed a chocolatier though.

PAULINE EYRE

....

What are librarians' favourite chocolate bars? Wispas.

JENAN YOUNIS

....

HOME

BABIES

It doesn't matter how many times you insult a baby, they always come crawling back.

ADELE CLIFF

....

No one wanted to come into the café after some toddlers spread their ice creams over everything. In fact, the whole place was desserted.

RICHARD PULSFORD

....

After watching my baby crawl and stagger around the room I was really proud when he took his first steps. And now he's admitted that he's got a problem, we're hoping it won't be long before he's off the bottle completely!

PHILIP SIMON

....

My sex education teacher gave us all a big piece of fruit to look after over a weekend as if it were a baby. It was my daughter Melon.

KAT MOLINARI

....

You know what gets on my tits? Starving babies.

LOVDEV BARPAGA

....

I can't for the life of me remember the name
of the fictional baby-delivery system,
it's driving me stork raving mad!

CHRIS NORTON WALKER

. . . .

They say 'sleep when baby sleeps', but every
time I try, I keep drifting onto the hard shoulder.

ROB THOMAS

. . . .

Do you remember when having tantrums
was all the rage?

STEVIE VEGAS

. . . .

My blind date asked me why I was wearing nappies.
I replied, 'You told me you were expecting a baby.'

JOSEPH MURPHY

. . . .

Boris Johnson can never seem to remember
how many children he has had. I think he
must suffer from pramnesia.

ANDREW TYMMS

. . . .

I wanted to find out what the noise was my baby
was making so I had to google 'ga ga'.

IAIN MACDONALD

. . . .

**Who called them 'Childproof Caps'
and not 'Baby Seals'?**

MASAI GRAHAM

....

**My friends have just had their first child, 8 lb 7oz,
stupid name for a baby if you ask me.**

TONY COWARDS

....

**My wife wants to get a bouncer for our newborn's
nursery but I said no. I think the last thing our
daughter needs is someone drinking Red Bull
at her bedroom door all night.**

SEAN HEGARTY

....

**Our baby's first words were 'E=mc^2'
– we'd just moved her on to formula.**

KEVIN HUDSON

....

**I'd be so excited if I could be like a baby and
cry when I wanted. Well up for that.**

PAUL SAVAGE

....

**My friends' baby was born on 20 December.
They had a nappy Christmas.**

HENRY DAWE

....

We left our baby on a doorstep. He's self-raising.

DARREN WALSH

....

My baby had a sore bum. My husband wanted to treat it with cream, but I thought that was a little rash.

PAULINE EYRE

....

The church is getting delivery of a new font. I can't wait for the Courier.

RICHARD PULSFORD

....

From the moment my son was born, I wanted to send him back, just to tidy his womb!

PHILIP SIMON

....

There's a baby ballroom dancing competition in the South West countryside. It's the cot's waltz.

KAT MOLINARI

....

My book on 42-week pregnancy is way overdue.

CHRIS NORTON WALKER

....

My baby is amazing. It's what gets me out of bed in the morning.

ROB THOMAS

....

If a lady ever tells you that her next baby will emerge sideways, I'd give her a wide berth.

STEVIE VEGAS

....

I handed my mum her sixtieth birthday card today. She said, 'One would've been enough.'

JOSEPH MURPHY

....

What do you say to a designer baby? Gucci, Gucci, Goo.

ANDREW TYMMS

....

The lady in my local kebab shop is pregnant. Soon she will be hearing the pitta-patter of tiny feet. I think her name is Donna.

IAIN MACDONALD

....

I thought the word 'caesarean' began with the letter 'S' but when I looked in the dictionary it was in the 'C' section.

MASAI GRAHAM

....

I once helped to deliver a baby – well, the postman was struggling to get it through the letterbox.

TONY COWARDS

....

I never thought in a million years that I would be able to build a Jack-in-the-box. I surprise myself sometimes.

DARREN WALSH

....

My wife said that I'd be in big trouble if I eat any more of my baby daughter's biscuits. But, hey, that's a Rusk I'm willing to take.

SEAN HEGARTY

....

Our baby just fitted the windows in our house. She's putty trained.

KEVIN HUDSON

....

Shout out to breastfeeding women. Keep on expressing yourselves

PAUL SAVAGE

....

On Wednesday, a mother of six had her seventh child and commented that he was her fattest baby yet. She said she'd never given anyone such a wide birth.

HENRY DAWE

....

I'm 18 months pregnant, but nobody wants to talk about it. That'll be the elephant in the womb.

PAULINE EYRE

....

CHILDREN

When I was in school my favourite branch of mathematics was the one where you calculate swine over cos. Pigonometry.

ADELE CLIFF

....

My mother was a poor swimmer and always wanted me to hold her in the pool, which is why I was called a mummy's buoy.

RICHARD PULSFORD

....

I've got a children's book on the history of the Internet, it's full of pop-ups.

RICHARD WOOLFORD

....

Ideas are like children – the better they turn out, the more people suspect they weren't yours in the first place!

PHILIP SIMON

....

My son earns his pocket money by cleaning the floors. He's my moppet.

KAT MOLINARI

....

If you have a baby in space, just rocket to sleep.

CHRIS NORTON WALKER

....

When I was a child, I was raised by a couple
who were always drinking Australian lager.
They were more like my foster parents.

COLIN LEGGO

....

Something tells me it was cruel of
us to name him 'Something'.

ROB THOMAS

....

Went to the rubbish tip earlier. There was a
sign that said 'KEEP CHILDREN IN CAR',
but I don't have any children.

STEVIE VEGAS

....

I tried doing comedy to Peter Pan and the Lost Boys,
but my jokes never land.

JOSEPH MURPHY

....

A group of nursery school pupils planted
some chocolate eggs with toys in them.
It was a Kinder garden.

IAIN MACDONALD

....

My dad is from Jamaica and my mum is from Wales.
That makes me the black sheep of the family.

MASAI GRAHAM

. . . .

To pass the time we got the children to dress up
as ABBA, the youngest didn't know who he was
supposed to be. Honestly, kids today, they
don't even know they're Björn.

TONY COWARDS

. . . .

My teacher told me to make a vacuum
and I thought, *No pressure then*.

LEO KEARSE

. . . .

Got drunk, went dancing, came home and
told my son that he wasn't getting any
inheritance. I really let my heir down.

DARREN WALSH

. . . .

I bought my son a jigsaw for his birthday
because, let's face it, that laminate floor's
not going to cut itself!

SEAN HEGARTY

. . . .

Bob the Builder's boss was George the Foreman.

KEVIN HUDSON

. . . .

My son had some good news, and his imaginary friend was very happy for him. He's made up.

PAUL SAVAGE

....

My little boy is mad on football so I'm hoping to get him what he has secretly told me he really wants: the autographs of Gary and Phil Neville. I'm just going to try Gary, though, because we've at least met over the years, whereas I've never even spoken to Phil. And after all, it's better the Neville you know than the Neville you don't.

HENRY DAWE

....

I was an odd child at school — I was interested in things like the Chinese Communist Party or depicting logical relationships. It was a long time ago, but I still think of it, Mao and Venn.

SEAN PATRICK

....

Childhood's really fun. Especially when you first discover poo sticks ... to everything.

PAULINE EYRE

....

My sister has two children, one's a boy and one's a girl. I think the girl's the niece-est.

ADELE CLIFF

....

So, I had the kids in the kitchen before I left. And they said to me, 'Dad? What are you making us squeeze all these oranges for?' I said, 'Concentrate!'

RICHARD PULSFORD

On our first date my wife told me she couldn't bear children. We've got two sons now, and it turns out I can't stand kids either!

PHILIP SIMON

What's the youngest part of Egypt's largest river called? The juvenile.

KAT MOLINARI

I stole my kid's pram, she'll come crawling back.

CHRIS NORTON WALKER

When I was a kid and my parents separated, they felt so guilty that they bought me loads of garden playing equipment, so swings and roundabouts.

COLIN LEGGO

I'd love to be a nit-nurse. That's a job that boxes all the ticks.

ROB THOMAS

Saw a sign saying 'PLEASE SLOW DOWN CHILDREN CROSSING'. Managed to trip a couple of them up as the rest ran past. Glad to have helped.

STEVIE VEGAS

....

My son has opened up a falafel shop.
I awake to the pitta platter of tiny Pete.

JOSEPH MURPHY

....

In splitting up your large Lego bricks between your two children, you have to be duplomatic.

IAIN MACDONALD

....

As a child I never beat my dad at conkers.
When I found out he used my grandfather's
one, I thought, *That old chestnut.*

MASAI GRAHAM

....

I always hated Take Your Child to Work Day as a kid because both my parents were teachers.

TONY COWARDS

....

'My nephew would like to borrow
your *Toy Story* costume.'
'Oh, Woody?'

DARREN WALSH

....

My nine-year-old son is too cool for school.
But, according to social services, 'That's not
a legitimate reason to keep him off!'

SEAN HEGARTY

. . . .

I couldn't believe it when I found out that a
former British newspaper is being revived both
by children, and for children. *Kids' Today*.

LAURA MONMOTH

. . . .

I always get up an hour before sunrise,
but then my son's a lazy so-and-so.

KEVIN HUDSON

. . . .

Kid Gloves: the youngest gangster in Chicago.

HENRY DAWE

. . . .

All week my children have been asking for stuff,
expensive stuff: a woman with a parasol, a beach,
water lilies. They must think I'm made of Monet.

SEAN PATRICK

. . . .

Online school means my kids don't even have to
pick up a pencil, let alone walk to school.
It's just stationery.

PAULINE EYRE

. . . .

PETS

I ordered a goose online but was sent a pelican.
I knew something was up when I saw the
size of the bill.

RICHARD PULSFORD

....

Vets and their small mammal thermometers,
they're always up ferret.

ADELE CLIFF

....

My dog goes, 'Booyaka, booyaka',
he's a Junglist Mastiff.

RICHARD WOOLFORD

....

The vet said my dog needed a shot. I said 'Tequila?'
He said, 'No, hopefully this should keep her alive!'

PHILIP SIMON

....

One day, my hamster was so lonely he ate loads of
nuts and seeds, put on some music and danced
with himself, cheek to cheek.

ROB THOMAS

....

My cat's surgeon is an army vet.
By that, I mean he has extremely large biceps.

KAT MOLINARI

. . . .

What's your pet hate? Mostly me, not feeding it.

CHRIS NORTON WALKER

. . . .

Apparently, all cats secretly collect albums by
Eminem or Jay-Z but every dog does have his Dre.

COLIN LEGGO

. . . .

While my lizard was being kept in overnight at the
vet's (it had a reptile dysfunction), they were kind
enough to give me a courtesy cat.

STEVIE VEGAS

. . . .

'What do we want?'

'More balls of string!'

'When do we want it?'

'Meow.'

JOSEPH MURPHY

. . . .

PETS

Guess what my girlfriend bought me for my
birthday this year? A talking dog. Says a lot!

ANDREW TYMMS

....

When a cat gets hurt, it makes a noise like me: 'ow'.

IAIN MACDONALD

....

I went to a German pet cemetery.
All of the cats had *nein* lives.

MASAI GRAHAM

....

My dog is a rescue dog, which is great, except when
he gets called out in the middle of the night.

TONY COWARDS

....

In Iran everyone's scared of spiders
but in Iraq, no phobia.

LEO KEARSE

....

My dog isn't sure whether he's broccoli or not.
He's a border cauliflower.

DARREN WALSH

....

I'm currently reading a book about a sick dog.
I can't put it down.

SEAN HEGARTY

....

My parrot isn't speaking to me after I forgot to feed him yesterday. Now, who's a petty boy then?

GRAHAM MUSK

....

I called my new dog Katie Hopkins. It's my pet hate.

LAURA MONMOTH

....

Every time a bell rang, Pavlova's dogs would eat raspberries, cream and meringue.

KEVIN HUDSON

....

I've met the man who decides what goes into pet food, and fair play to him. That takes a lot of bollocks.

PAUL SAVAGE

....

Yorkshire Terrier: a dog with two 'i's.

HENRY DAWE

....

My mate used to keep tortoises and terrapins. I asked him how he could tell which was which. Apparently, it's easy, they're turtley different.

NIGEL LOVELL

....

My snake loves cleaning car windows, he's a windscreen viper.

RICHARD WOOLFORD

....

'I get up when I want to, except every single morning, when I'm rudely awakened by two elephants having sex in a confined space.' Noah's 'Arklife'.

SEAN PATRICK

....

My friend said her cat had a litter of 12. I said, 'You're kitten me!' She also said her goat had 14 babies, so I knew she was kidding.

PAULINE EYRE

....

At school I was a teacher's pet, which meant I had to go home with a different member of the class every weekend.

ADELE CLIFF

....

Kirk Douglas hated how smug his cat was. In the end he was like, 'No! I'm smarter, Puss!'

PHILIP SIMON

....

There's a *Shrek* spin-off where the cat becomes a therapist. *Discuss in Boots*.

KAT MOLINARI

....

Someone repossessed all of my exotic pets, glad I got that monkey off my back.

CHRIS NORTON WALKER

....

When my pet gerbil died I took him to a taxidermist, and she quoted me five grand. I said, 'Yeah? You can stuff that then.'

RICHARD PULSFORD

....

When they're in Rome, Labradors aren't allowed to go and watch the gladiators but the Collies see 'em.

COLIN LEGGO

....

While we were on holiday my mother and father-in-law looked after our two cats. One of them was sick on the carpet, but at least the cats behaved.

ROB THOMAS

....

My cats enjoy drinking hot beverages then coughing them up again. It's hairball tea.

STEVIE VEGAS

....

I got this shampoo that makes my hair smell like a pet shop, it's called Gerbil Essences.

LEO KEARSE

....

The police are looking for someone who keeps releasing all the dogs from the kennel. They don't have any leads.

JOSEPH MURPHY

....

I've spent too much on pet birds again.
I've gone way over budgie.

ANDREW TYMMS

....

You got to feel sorry for German cats,
what with having *nein* lives.

IAIN MACDONALD

....

I don't know why the Queen has so many corgis as
Buckingham Palace has enough unwanted heirs.

MASAI GRAHAM

....

Starting to get fed up with the cat's constant
scratching, beginning to wish I'd never
taught him to DJ.

TONY COWARDS

....

Marvin Gaye used to keep a sheep in my vineyard.
He'd herd it through the grapevine.

LEO KEARSE

....

I got a new dog and discovered that instead of a
tongue, it had a piece of flatbread in its mouth.
It was then I knew I had the lick of the pitta.

LAURA MONMOTH

....

Had some shellfish thank me for identifying them.
I said, 'No probs, you're whelks.'

PAUL SAVAGE

....

If I take my cat to the vet, he dies.
If I take him home, he dies. Cat's 22.

DARREN WALSH

....

I auditioned recently for a movie about a lost dog.
I got the lead!

SEAN HEGARTY

....

A Basset Hound is a hound that eats liquorice allsorts.

KEVIN HUDSON

....

You can lead a dyslexic horse to Walter.

PAUL SAVAGE

....

We're going to buy a livelier pet next time, not like
that slow old creature we had before. That's one
thing our last decision taught us.

HENRY DAWE

....

The pet shop was closed,
but I broke in and took a Peke.

PAULINE EYRE

....

'I'm taking my pet bird on holiday with me this year.'

'Carrier pigeon?'

'No chance, he's got wings. Let him fly.'

SEAN PATRICK

· · · · · · · · · · · · · · · · · · · ·

I lost my pet snake the other day. I should be more careful as they're talented escape artists that can eviperate into thin air!

JENAN YOUNIS

· · · · · · · · · · · · · · · · · · · ·

MISCELLANEOUS

HEALTH

The NHS have run out of plasters.
The government are blaming it on all the cuts.

PHILIP SIMON

....

My friend is a plastic surgeon
but they prefer the term body builder.

ADELE CLIFF

....

I've just had a health check and apart from my
deafness getting worse I was relieved to hear the
only other thing I have is some gentle warts.

RICHARD PULSFORD

....

Those people on life support are rude, aren't
they? Always swearing, it's just 'beep this'
and 'beep that' with them.

RICHARD WOOLFORD

....

My diabetic friend and I first met because I
handed her my Lucozade while she had a
hypoglycaemia attack. We glucose after that.

KAT MOLINARI

....

Since I became a below-knee amputee, I've discovered I can no longer drink milk. I'm lack toes intolerant.

COLIN LEGGO

....

Circumcision improves hygiene no end.

ROB THOMAS

....

Need to visit the optician's as my boss said that I require super vision.

STEVIE VEGAS

....

I won't rest till I find a cure for insomnia.

JOSEPH MURPHY

....

My brother has got coeliac disease and yet he continues to eat products containing wheat. He's such a gluten for punishment.

ANDREW TYMMS

....

If you are selfish and need stitches, you need to suture self.

IAIN MACDONALD

....

My dad was really nervous about his upcoming blood test, so I said to him, 'Be positive.'

MASAI GRAHAM

....

Every week I see a hypnotist to help me work out why I'm losing all my money. Halfway through the last session I realised the answer was staring me in the face.

ROB THOMAS

. . . .

My proctologist is a very lazy man, sometimes I just wish he'd pull his finger out.

TONY COWARDS

. . . .

If some guy chucks a milkshake at me, he'll be drinking his next milkshake through a straw.

LEO KEARSE

. . . .

Does your nan like spicy chicken? My nan does.

LEO KEARSE

. . . .

I watch ghost movies while sitting in a bath full of yogurt – I like to dabble in the Yakult.

LEO KEARSE

. . . .

I went to A&E because I believed I was a New York actor who danced in a Fatboy Slim video. It wasn't serious so they sent me to the Walken centre.

LAURA MONMOTH

. . . .

I heard a sneeze from the chimney. I think
Santa's coming down with something.

DARREN WALSH

. . . .

I've started picking my nose more.
The doctor said I need to eat my greens.

SEAN HEGARTY

. . . .

Private medical cover is all about health cheques.

KEVIN HUDSON

. . . .

I'm happy to spread happiness.
What's dopamine is dopayours.

PAUL SAVAGE

. . . .

A popular book among the medical
profession is *Lady Chatterley's Liver*.

HENRY DAWE

. . . .

Some people claim the coughing fit that killed
my grandfather was caused by the strong cigarettes
he smoked, but it was actually a piece of roast
pheasant. So, I say to them, 'Don't hate
the Players. Hate the game.'

SEAN PATRICK

. . . .

My mate can't stop reading about Amy Johnson, Florence Nightingale and Joan of Arc. Very sad, but that's heroine addiction.

NIGEL LOVELL

....

Did you hear about the man who put 1,000 pound coins up his bum? He had piles of money.

PAULINE EYRE

....

The surgeon said to me I'll live but I'll have a urostomy for the rest of my life. I told him: 'You must be taking the piss!'

JENAN YOUNIS

....

My yoga instructor says if I want to find enlightenment I need to look inside myself, but it's the beginners' class and I'm not that flexible yet.

ADELE CLIFF

....

Tried to swim a length in an infinity pool, it took forever.

CHRIS NORTON WALKER

....

Why didn't Santa have any helpers in 2020? They were all in Elf isolation.

RICHARD WOOLFORD

....

The patient next to me in A&E, who had a pen
stuck up her nose, asked me what I was in for.
I said, 'Don't be such a nosy parker.'

RICHARD PULSFORD

....

I refused to own up to my partner that I needed to
take his advice and go to hospital about my broken
toes. In the end though, I had to admit da feet.

KAT MOLINARI

....

My dad's glasses keep making him see green ogres.
Should have gone to Shreksavers.

COLIN LEGGO

....

Dentist has put my teeth in a brace. Now they
can stop my trousers from falling down.

STEVIE VEGAS

....

My doctor has advised me to stop running,
after I stole his stethoscope.

JOSEPH MURPHY

....

When it comes to diets, there are two groups
of people: the dos and the donuts.

ANDREW TYMMS

....

I share a car when going to work but my wrists get really numb and tingly whenever we go through an underpass. It's carpool tunnel syndrome.

IAIN MACDONALD

. . . .

My dad suggested I register for a donor card. He's a man after my own heart.

MASAI GRAHAM

. . . .

My doctor has told me that all my internal organs are enlarged, and I say that with a very heavy heart.

TONY COWARDS

. . . .

I've just been diagnosed with kleptomania. My psychiatrist said that if I need anything, her door is always open.

DARREN WALSH

. . . .

One of my friends cut himself on a really old photograph and now he's got sepiacemia.

GRAHAM MUSK

. . . .

I suffered from inflammation of my stomach that could only be cured by smoking large cigars. It was Castroenteritis.

LAURA MONMOTH

. . . .

I had to collect my dad from the maternity ward this morning. Apparently, he'd been trying to deliver babies while wearing a nurse's uniform. He can't help it though; he's going through a mid-wife crisis.

SEAN HEGARTY

. . . .

My wife gave me a tablet for my birthday.
I've not taken it yet.

KEVIN HUDSON

. . . .

I'm worried about how much fluid I'm ejaculating, but that's a problem I will overcome.

PAUL SAVAGE

. . . .

Had some good news, and my imaginary friend is happy for me. He's made up.

PAUL SAVAGE

. . . .

As I lay dying, my life flashed before my eyes, creating a strobe effect and setting off my epilepsy.

PAUL SAVAGE

. . . .

I'm not convinced my doctor really has my best interests at heart. He's prescribed me wax tablets.

HENRY DAWE

. . . .

I used to work as a demonstrator for Optrex.
That was an eye-opener.

NIGEL LOVELL

....

My mum's been put on MRT to help with the
menopause. It's like HRT but, instead of just coping
with the symptoms, she pities the fools.

SEAN PATRICK

....

To be a chiropodist, you need a pod degree;
to be a urologist, you need a pee degree;
and bakers need a pud degree.

PAULINE EYRE

....

I got the Pfizer COVID-19 vaccine the other day.
The nurse said my arm might feel a little sore
afterwards, but I was absolutely Pfine.

JENAN YOUNIS

....

CARTOONS

I saw Fred and Wilma smoking a joint. They were getting Flinstoned, it was a yabba dabba doobie.

ADELE CLIFF

....

My old Looney Tunes app still has Bugs in it.

RICHARD PULSFORD

....

I got my haircut by Fred Fintstone,
it's a yabba dabba doo.

RICHARD WOOLFORD

....

I like to draw pictures of Ned Flanders
whenever I'm feeling a bit doodly.

KAT MOLINARI

....

I went down to the Great Barrier Reef and met
a cartoon dog. He was Scooby diving.

COLIN LEGGO

....

Which cartoon hero can't stop laughing?
He-He-He-Man.

ANDREW TYMMS

....

I love the Disney movie where a girl realises her weight issues have nothing to do with her looks: *Beauty and Obese.*

PHILIP SIMON

....

I think that a group from Warner Brothers have planted some listening devices in my kitchen. I'm having to sweep the room for bugs.

STEVIE VEGAS

....

Baloo the bear asked where he could find cheap jewellery. I said, 'Look for the Claire's Accessories.'

JOSEPH MURPHY

....

I never understood Scrappy Doo's catchphrase about heavy-rock singers' molecule obsession. Lemme atom, lemme atom.

IAIN MACDONALD

....

Spider-Man's catchphrase should've been, 'That's my storey and I'm sticking to it.'

MASAI GRAHAM

....

All Pixar films should come with the warning, 'Contains graphic scenes'.

TONY COWARDS

....

I get my cartoon suits from Popeye the tailor man.

KEVIN HUDSON

....

Gameshow Host: **What is the main ingredient when making pizza?**

Homer: **Cheese.**

Gameshow Host: **No!**

Homer: **Doh!**

Gameshow Host: **Correct!**

SEAN HEGARTY

....

The Flintstones **made a lot of money on the Russian stock market. Betty Ruble.**

LAURA MONMOTH

....

I borrowed money off one of the Simpsons. I got a Homer loan.

KEVIN HUDSON

....

Slow-walking *Lion King* character? I was like Mufasa!

CHRIS NORTON WALKER

....

**If Catwoman decided to go to Nepal,
what would Catman do?**

DARREN WALSH

. . . .

**I'm asking my friends if they'll draw cartoons
for me. Annie May shunned the idea.**

PAULINE EYRE

. . . .

**I recently saw a Japanese cartoon about a
webbed superhero. It was *Spider-Manime*.**

ADELE CLIFF

. . . .

**My ready meal said, 'Cook from frozen', and I thought,
I don't remember that character in the film.**

RICHARD PULSFORD

. . . .

**Buzz Lightyear loves it when body parts of
sharks are pleasing in their proportions.
To fin symmetry and beyond!**

COLIN LEGGO

. . . .

***Tom & Jerry* cartoons were very tame.
It wasn't till they introduced the dog character
that there was a spike in the violence.**

MASAI GRAHAM

. . . .

My friend has an extreme irrational hatred of the dad from *The Simpsons*, he's Homerphobic.

RICHARD WOOLFORD

....

There's a new Disney-themed witness protection scheme called Lie Low and Snitch.

PHILIP SIMON

....

Went to a charity event where a bunch of stand-ups got their kit off. It was a comic strip.

KAT MOLINARI

....

I cleaned my house with 101 Dalmatians. Now it is spotless!

STEVIE VEGAS

....

Which Looney Tunes character can always be found hiding out in the graveyard? Yo Cemetery Sam.

ANDREW TYMMS

....

I phoned Sky recently to complain about the Boomerang channel. Every time I try to turn over, it keeps turning back.

SEAN HEGARTY

....

The bear from *The Jungle Book* all of a sudden started swearing at me. It came completely out of the Baloo.

IAIN MACDONALD

. . . .

I get very cross when I watch Japanese cartoons. Apparently, I have a problem with my manga management.

TONY COWARDS

. . . .

I'm to guest star in an episode of *The Simpsons*. I didn't plan it, I just got drawn in.

DARREN WALSH

. . . .

The creators of Yogi Bear had no idea what to call his girlfriend. They were Cindycisive.

LAURA MONMOTH

. . . .

Mickey Mouse: cartoon character who has had the mickey taken out of him.

HENRY DAWE

. . . .

I looked up Charles M. Schulz on Cartoon Networth – turns out he was paid peanuts.

PAULINE EYRE

. . . .

TIME

A newspaper once ran a series of articles by Stephen
Hawking on underwear through the ages. It was
called *The Times* 'History of Briefs'.

RICHARD PULSFORD

. . . .

The hypnotist wants to charge me £500 just
for telling me I was Swedish in a past life.
He must think I was Björn yesterday.

RICHARD PULSFORD

. . . .

The BBC asked Brian Cox to host a political
panel show, but he said one thing he
would never do was *Question Time*.

PHILIP SIMON

. . . .

The best television shows are on at two, three, five,
seven and eleven o'clock. That's prime time!

PHILIP SIMON

. . . .

Whenever my sister explains to me how long ago
the nineties was, I just pretend I can't era.

KAT MOLINARI

. . . .

I lost a friend recently because we had a disagreement about the TARDIS, which I thought was just a little thing, but it turned out to be much bigger once we got into it.

ADELE CLIFF

....

There's a tree in America that grows nickels after a hundred years of being alive. It's a cent tree.

KAT MOLINARI

....

I always put a clock in my beehive. Time is honey.

CHRIS NORTON WALKER

....

I used to work in a carriage clock factory. Wasn't really that difficult, just ticking boxes.

CHRIS NORTON WALKER

....

Apparently, Obama has built a time machine specifically to visit the year 1985. Barack to the Future.

COLIN LEGGO

....

I'm currently writing a book on how Professor Stephen Hawking's underwear loved talking about old clocks. *A Brief History of Time*.

COLIN LEGGO

....

I'm ready to deliver an important presentation about that noise that a watch makes. Tune in tonight for my tick-tock TED Talk.

STEVIE VEGAS

....

When I try to throw my alarm clock to the ground in the morning, a guy with big gloves appears and manages to save it. He's my time keeper.

STEVIE VEGAS

....

'My watch hasn't worked in— I'm not sure how long.'

JOSEPH MURPHY

....

I bought a really expensive digital watch. I regretted it literally a minute later.

JOSEPH MURPHY

....

When is the best time to visit a cash point in America? ATM.

ANDREW TYMMS

....

We wanted to name our dog after a unit of time, but we took so long in deciding, we eventually had to call it a day.

IAIN MACDONALD

....

When I wash the dishes, I love to dance.
My feet are all over the place but at least
my hands are in sink.

IAIN MACDONALD

....

I hung my spice rack opposite my mirror
and now I've got thyme to reflect.

MASAI GRAHAM

....

Why didn't Michael J. Fox take out a pension?
He turned his back to the future.

MASAI GRAHAM

....

Jokes about time travel are so next year.

TONY COWARDS

....

I came last in a recent watch-making competition
for showing up with missing parts. To make matters
worse, the MC announced, 'He finished rock bottom
but that doesn't matter, let's give him a big hand!'

SEAN HEGARTY

....

My boss said she'd been in back-to-back meetings
all day, so I told her that the meetings would be
more productive if people faced each other.

LEO KEARSE

....

224

My new alarm clock is perfect for networking,
it's got a schmooze button.

TONY COWARDS

....

What time does a Chinese man go to the dentist?
Any time he wants, it's not the seventies.

LEO KEARSE

....

Superficial people are sooo last year.

DARREN WALSH

....

My girlfriend keeps asking me the time,
precisely to the nearest one-sixtieth of a minute.
I think she's using me for secs.

DARREN WALSH

....

It took me four years but I'm proud to say that I've
finally finished my book about Big Ben. I know
what you're thinking, it's about time.

SEAN HEGARTY

....

The people of south-east London hate when the
clocks go back. It's their Greenwich Moan Time.

LAURA MONMOTH

....

I've got no herbs left. I ran out of thyme.

KEVIN HUDSON

....

I've got a load of dead watch batteries
that I'm giving away, free of charge.

PAUL SAVAGE

....

I shall never understand my wife's propensity to arrive
late for everything. It will always be a mystery to me,
the relationship between Rosemary and time.

HENRY DAWE

....

Sir Ken Dodd was once billed as 'Liverpool's Latest
Comedian'. And believe me, when you emerged from
the theatre and saw the milkman driving home, you
realised that they didn't come much later than Doddy.

HENRY DAWE

....

When you live your life on hammer time,
every month is Stoptober.

SEAN PATRICK

....

Finally got my chest freezer delivered this
afternoon. My chest is now three hours
younger than the rest of me.

SEAN PATRICK

....

He cuts himself way less since
he discovered daylight shaving time.

PAULINE EYRE

. . . .

I went to see my friend's daughter's nativity play.
To be honest, I couldn't tell which one she was,
'cause I haven't seen her for donkey's ears.

PAULINE EYRE

. . . .

A parsec is 3.262 light years, but you can travel
a Nicholas Parsec in just a minute.

FRIZ FRIZZLE

. . . .

I got a Rolex for my birthday but it turned out
to be a fake. It was a right wind-up.

JENAN YOUNIS

. . . .

THE WEATHER

I once met a vegan vampire, who sucks the
nectar from plants. The Pollen Count.

ADELE CLIFF

....

Managed to capture a storm.
Now experiencing trapped wind.

STEVIE VEGAS

....

Weather presenters are normally drunk because they
spend so much time hanging around in iso-bars.

ADELE CLIFF

....

Being with my cheating ex was like having my own
thunder catcher. They were always getting the clap.

KAT MOLINARI

....

I once saw a weatherman wee himself
live on air, talk about a warm front.

CHRIS NORTON WALKER

....

I love songs about cheese in June and July
– 'Summer Bries make me feel fine!'

CHRIS NORTON WALKER

....

Maybe a dozen local parks have lost much of
their grass in the recent dry spell, though
that's just a bald park figure.

RICHARD PULSFORD

. . . .

When I'm ill in the winter, I like to write songs
about never dropping cough sweets. The singing
isn't good but I can hold a Tune.

COLIN LEGGO

. . . .

Have you heard Prince's song about the German
chancellor having a wee? 'Merkel rain, Merkel rain.'

ROB THOMAS

. . . .

I've just become a manager at a snow globe factory.
Time to shake things up.

JOSEPH MURPHY

. . . .

My first stage show, *Rain*, was an absolute disaster.
There were far more actors than there were roles.
It was completely overcast.

ANDREW TYMMS

. . . .

How do you know that all weather forecasters
are carnivores? They are all meat-eater ologists.

IAIN MACDONALD

. . . .

My umbrella is useless in the wind, as it turns out.

MASAI GRAHAM

. . . .

Hot weather always makes me feel like a rock star, every night I sleep with a fan.

TONY COWARDS

. . . .

Did you know what raincoats are made in Iran? An Iraq.

DARREN WALSH

. . . .

I got disqualified from the UK Weatherman Championships in the semi-finals, for being *too* obsessed with the weather. You know what they say though, it's not the winning that counts, it's the precipitation.

SEAN HEGARTY

. . . .

Why was the knife saying it was going to rain today? Because its fork asked!

GRAHAM MUSK

. . . .

After they retire, all television weather presenters get sent to a really horrible island in the South Pacific. It's known as the Bilge Isles.

LAURA MONMOTH

. . . .

We flew to Spain and it rained all the way till we got
off. Then it was brilliant sunshine. That's because
the rain in Spain stays mainly on the plane.

KEVIN HUDSON

....

Friend 1: I loved *That Was the Week That Was* –
brilliantly fronted by Peter Snow.

Friend 2: It wasn't Peter Snow. It was David Frost.

Friend 3: Are you sure it wasn't John Thaw?

HENRY DAWE

....

Why is it you'll never find a vegetarian weatherman?
Because they are all meaterologists.

JENAN YOUNIS

....

I was surprised to see a line of North Africans
out in the snow today eating grilled food as it
wasn't exactly Berber-queuing weather.

RICHARD PULSFORD

....

'Oven. Crinkle Cut. Golf Shot.
That was the *Chipping News* from the BBC.'

PHILIP SIMON

....

The Weather Girls have re-recorded their
1982 hit and made it about yoga teachers
instead – 'It's Raining Zen'.

KAT MOLINARI

. . . .

The new weatherman took over the rains.

CHRIS NORTON WALKER

. . . .

Did you know it can only rain if there's more than two
people. As they say, 'two's company, three's a cloud'.

COLIN LEGGO

. . . .

Gene Kelly calling from a boat in Paris:
'I'm ringing in the Seine.'

ROB THOMAS

. . . .

Managed to win a game that was about who
could cause the most downpour from the skies.
I am now the raining champion.

STEVIE VEGAS

. . . .

I checked the weather forecast and I think it said
that emails should expect rain. No, wait,
it said the outlook was cloudy.

IAIN MACDONALD

. . . .

It's been raining cats and dogs.
It never rains, but it paws.

ANDREW TYMMS

....

During lockdown I found time to find the
difference between *nimbus*, *stratus*, *cumulus*
and *cirrus*. So, every cloud...

MASAI GRAHAM

....

Woke up early this morning, no idea where the
sun had gone and then it dawned on me.

TONY COWARDS

....

I came out of the sunbed with a pink head,
a yellow torso and brown legs. It was a Neapolitan.

DARREN WALSH

....

I've just binge-watched *The Northern Irish Weather*
on Netflix. All four seasons in one day.

SEAN HEGARTY

....

'You talking to me? You talking to me? Then who else
are you talking to? You talking to me? Well, I'm the
only weather phenomenon here!' – El Niro

LAURA MONMOTH

....

Have you seen the overcast TV presenter?
Cloudier Winkleman.

KEVIN HUDSON

....

Jesus: What on earth is that weather outside?
I've never seen anything like it.

Disciple: It's hail, the heaven-born Prince
of Peace; hail, the Son of Righteousness.

HENRY DAWE

....

The fisherman was asked if he preferred to work in the
sunshine. He said, 'No, I'm a cloudier winkle man.'
I then asked him if he strictly adhered to quality
control standards and he replied, 'Yes, I test daily.'

PAULINE EYRE

....

WEDDINGS

I proposed to my girlfriend at the local duck pond.
I got down on one knee.

RICHARD PULSFORD

. . . .

I bought my wife some Slinky underwear,
now she keeps falling down the stairs.

RICHARD WOOLFORD

. . . .

My optimistic friend wasn't sure whether to get
married locally or abroad. I guess elope for the best.

PHILIP SIMON

. . . .

I had an orchestra for my wedding but they all had
a broken arm each. It was a sling quartet.

KAT MOLINARI

. . . .

My wife has big ears and a metallic complexion,
she's a trophy wife.

CHRIS NORTON WALKER

. . . .

Last time I entertained at a wedding, it seemed
to go without a hitch, which was unfortunate.

STEVIE VEGAS

. . . .

To impress my 80-year-old girlfriend at our wedding, I turned up dressed as a JCB painted with a precious metal. Now she thinks I'm a gold digger.

COLIN LEGGO

．．．．．．．．．．．．．．．．．．

When I told my fiancée that I had booked our honeymoon in Outer Space, she was over the moon.

STEVIE VEGAS

．．．．．．．．．．．．．．．．．．

I bumped into my imaginary ex-wife today. It was awkward as I've started seeing someone else.

JOSEPH MURPHY

．．．．．．．．．．．．．．．．．．

My cousin was engaged to marry an electrician. I went to their wedding. It was shocking. She was jolted at the altar.

ANDREW TYMMS

．．．．．．．．．．．．．．．．．．

My wife has left me because of my pasta-touching fetish. I'm feeling cannelloni right now.

IAIN MACDONALD

．．．．．．．．．．．．．．．．．．

What will Kim Jong-un give his wife for their twentieth wedding anniversary? China.

MASAI GRAHAM

．．．．．．．．．．．．．．．．．．

I'm thinking about entering America's next
top model. She's really attractive.

LEO KEARSE

. . . .

I was in a band called the Tablecloths, but I left
because we only did covers at weddings.

DARREN WALSH

. . . .

The night before our wedding, my wife got cold feet.
Our chief bridesmaid bought her the box set.
Turns out she's a huge fan of James Nesbitt.

SEAN HEGARTY

. . . .

My friend didn't propose with a ring, instead he
got a set of crockery with Destiny's Child's faces
on the side. They're his fiancée bowls.

LAURA MONMOTH

. . . .

Standing at the altar, my wife said she was going
to kill me. It was a thinly veiled threat.

KEVIN HUDSON

. . . .

There's a hair and make-up lady who
only cuts blonde hair. Fair dos.

PAUL SAVAGE

. . . .

I was going to marry an Irishman, but he jilted me to go and live abroad. That was my ex, Pat.

SEAN PATRICK

....

The wedding company wanted to charge me £10 per head to put chocolates on the tables! I said, 'Do me a favour!'

PAULINE EYRE

....

My friends are trying to save money on their wedding, so I offered to do the bouquet. They weren't happy with the arrangement, which is a shame because it took me flowers.

ADELE CLIFF

....

For the last six months I've been going to classes with a top fashion designer. Now my fiancée wants me to make her wedding dress. I sincerely hope that I shall be able to pull it off.

HENRY DAWE

....

My friends are constantly trying to set me up with people at weddings, but I spend most of my time hiding behind flowers because I'm very socially orchid.

ADELE CLIFF

....

What's the favourite board game played by newly married Mormons? Monopolygamy.

JENAN YOUNIS

. . . .

My fiancée is the one in the pencil skirt. She's my bride 2B.

RICHARD PULSFORD

. . . .

Unfortunately, my first year as a wedding planner went off without a hitch.

PHILIP SIMON

. . . .

Everyone kept telling us we needed wedding insurance. Even our MC. In the end I was like, 'Go, compère!'

PHILIP SIMON

. . . .

I made my friend and his wife a repetitive animation of the moment they tied the knot. They loved my wedding gif.

PHILIP SIMON

. . . .

There's a cruise you can take that specialises in weddings. It's called the companion ship.

KAT MOLINARI

. . . .

During my wedding night I ironically got my
partner pregnant on a pull-out sofa.

CHRIS NORTON WALKER

....

I never showed up at my wedding to Miss Piggy.
I think I've got Kermitment issues.

COLIN LEGGO

....

I miss my ex-wife, she used to love counting
numbers. I wonder what she's up to now.

JOSEPH MURPHY

....

My sister married a bullfighter. I went to their
wedding – he promised to love, honour and *olé*!

ANDREW TYMMS

....

Did you hear about the premature ejaculator that
went into intensive care on his wedding night?
Apparently, it was touch and go.

IAIN MACDONALD

....

I've left my girlfriend at the altar three times.
She asked me if I actually wanted to get married and
I said, 'It's not that I don't, I just can't say I do.'

GRAHAM MUSK

....

I tried to arrange my wedding on the Ark,
but it was to Noah Veil.

MASAI GRAHAM

. . . .

When I lost the DVD of our wedding,
my wife ripped me a new one.

TONY COWARDS

. . . .

If a doe wants to celebrate her last night before
getting married, what does the stag do?

DARREN WALSH

. . . .

My girlfriend has a really weird foot fetish.
She keeps telling me, 'No socks before marriage!'

SEAN HEGARTY

. . . .

Two of my friends didn't want a normal wedding,
instead they spent hours throwing oranges at
each other. It was a Seville ceremony.

LAURA MONMOTH

. . . .

She thought I was proposing when I said,
'Shall I give you a ring sometime?'

KEVIN HUDSON

. . . .

Father of the Bride: And now, ladies and gentlemen, you will be relieved to hear that my speech is over, and the dancing may begin!

Mother of the Bride: What about the toast?

Father of the Bride: Haven't you had enough to eat?

HENRY DAWE

....

My name has been dragged through the mud at the hospital. Turns out you can't book a mammogram for a stag do.

SEAN PATRICK

....

When I was a bridesmaid, the bride wasn't bothered about my future. She didn't give a toss.

PAULINE EYRE

....

SOCIAL MEDIA

KFC have a blue tick on Twitter,
their chicken is very fried.

ADELE CLIFF

· · · · · · · · · · · · · · · · · · · ·

One of my professional connections suggested we talk
using two empty baked bean cans connected by
a piece of string. He actually still uses LinkTin.

RICHARD PULSFORD

· · · · · · · · · · · · · · · · · · · ·

I saw on Facebook my cousin's a bugler in the army.
I liked his Last Post.

PHILIP SIMON

· · · · · · · · · · · · · · · · · · · ·

I don't buy laundry detergent from brands that
have an 'about me' section on their Instagram
page. I prefer non-bio.

KAT MOLINARI

· · · · · · · · · · · · · · · · · · · ·

I wanted to visit that website where you leave
reviews about waiters but there's something
wrong with their server.

COLIN LEGGO

· · · · · · · · · · · · · · · · · · · ·

I keep posting about the COVID-19. That's right,
I do consider myself a social media influenza.

CHRIS NORTON WALKER

. . . .

Set up a new website rating the best fish suppers
I have ever eaten. It's called ChipAdvisor.

STEVIE VEGAS

. . . .

The creator of Spotify has been arrested.
The trial will last 30 days.

JOSEPH MURPHY

. . . .

After a family feud, my parents have unfriended
me and my brother on Facebook. I doubt we
will ever see their 'like' again.

ANDREW TYMMS

. . . .

I hate that I get Facebook ads for funky dancing
ex-vice presidents. I blame the dodgy algorerhythms.

IAIN MACDONALD

. . . .

The actor Danny John Jules was annoyed because he
couldn't work out who kept linking to his Facebook
page, but I soon let the cat out of the tag.

LAURA MONMOTH

. . . .

My nan keeps showing me baby photos
on her app, InstaGran.

LOVDEV BARPAGA

. . . .

I blocked my toilet last week. I don't know why I
accepted it's Facebook friend request in the first place.

MASAI GRAHAM

. . . .

Big news coming in about lots of celebrities
joining Twitter, more to follow.

TONY COWARDS

. . . .

I tried to watch a YouTube video of a car
being polished but it kept buffering.

DARREN WALSH

. . . .

My friend started crying after telling me that
his dead pet bird's got a social media account.
All I asked was what if it tweets?

SEAN HEGARTY

. . . .

Saw a very sad profile on Bumble earlier – a
woman whose life had been blighted by never fully
understanding how playing cards work. All those
wasted years, looking for the one.

SEAN PATRICK

. . . .

She said, 'Are you on Tinder?'
I said, 'No, I'm just naturally flammable.'

KEVIN HUDSON

....

I've got really into cancel culture
and now there's no more yogurt.

PAUL SAVAGE

....

More like social needier, am I right?

PAULINE EYRE

....

What makes viral tweets different?
They're superspreaders.

JENAN YOUNIS

....

My spam filter has stopped working,
now my inbox is full of processed meat.

ADELE CLIFF

....

Apple, they must make a huge turnover.

RICHARD PULSFORD

....

I see Cliff Richard is getting some online abuse,
he's got himself some lying, talking,
tweeting, stalking, living trolls.

RICHARD WOOLFORD

....

I recently posted a 280-character joke about how I've started breastfeeding again. Got loads of re-teets.

ADELE CLIFF

. . . .

I asked Bugs Bunny how he stayed in touch with all his friends. He said, 'Er ... WhatsApp, doc!'

PHILIP SIMON

. . . .

I once had a job thinking of cool Twitter names for people, but I couldn't handle it.

KAT MOLINARI

. . . .

After seeing an advert on social media, I bought some 'no more tears' shampoo but it did nothing for my depression.

CHRIS NORTON WALKER

. . . .

The new dating app I designed specifically for chickens started well but I'm struggling to make hens meet.

COLIN LEGGO

. . . .

I've been using the following chat-up line on Tinder: 'Hey girl, have you ever taken out a loan? Because I'm alone.'

JOSEPH MURPHY

. . . .

My computer keeps spraying me with men's deodorant every time I try to update my profile on Facebook. I think it's a Brut-force attack and I'm not able to click on any Lynx either.

STEVIE VEGAS

. . . .

I have just started on the Northern Twitter diet. It's a bit extreme. Nothing t'weet!

ANDREW TYMMS

. . . .

I don't like Internet Explorer or Firefox for logging into my social media accounts. I think they don't work as well as the Google one because they feel a bit rushed. That's cos Chrome wasn't built in a day.

IAIN MACDONALD

. . . .

I joined a fetish site for feeders; I had to accept their cookies.

LOVDEV BARPAGA

. . . .

The most used website in Morocco is Fezbook.

TONY COWARDS

. . . .

Someone called Tetris followed me on Twitter. I blocked him.

DARREN WALSH

. . . .

The Israeli prime minister told me not to email
him because he's not on Hotmail. I said,
'Ben, d'ya mean not on Yahoo?'

LEO KEARSE

....

I asked on Facebook for help to get onto the
London Stock Exchange. I couldn't believe it,
within minutes, I had five shares.

SEAN HEGARTY

....

I've set up a Facebook fan page for Tommy Cooper.
If you see it, just 'like' that.

EL BALDINHO

....

There's a blog on LinkedIn by one of the Two Ronnies
that has only ever been accessed by the pop star
Prince. It's a little read Corbett.

LAURA MONMOTH

....

If Elvis were alive today, he'd be
singing 'Love Me Tinder'.

KEVIN HUDSON

....

At first, I couldn't find TikTok in the list of social
media platforms online. Then I clocked it.

HENRY DAWE

....

Heartbroken. Updated my Tinder profile to include 'loves to travel' and now I've been blocked by the basketball coach I was chatting to.

SEAN PATRICK

. . . .

The FBI located the people who'd stormed the Capitol by milking Parler.

PAULINE EYRE

. . . .

How do social media influencers have their morning coffee? Filtered.

JENAN YOUNIS

. . . .

#UKPUNDAY

As you will hopefully already know, if you have read this book from the start, The UK Pun Championships was set up in 2014 to celebrate the Great British pun. The live contest takes place at De Montfort Hall as part of the annual Leicester Comedy Festival and more recently is broadcast live across the UK, courtesy of Union JACK Radio. At first, the silliness was pretty much confined to the sell-out show, with comedians, punsters and audience alike sharing the jokes and puns throughout the evening.

But then in 2016, after two years of sell-out shows, we decided to extend the pun, er the fun, across the UK (dare we even suggest across the world?!) with the introduction of #UKPunDay. Everyone in the country was invited to get on board the pun train, share punbelievable newspaper headlines, punspired shop names from around the country and shamelessly milk the cheers and groans that make punning excellent fun. Pundamentally, #UKPunday was introduced to extend the celebration of Britain's love of wordplay.

Many, many people have said the day was what Twitter was invented for. Short, funny messages that can be liked and shared among groups of friends. And it did seem to get off to a pretty good start. I remember the Friday before the first #UKPunDay, I emailed a few people I knew to remind them that it was happening and to encourage them to take part. Then on the morning of the first day, I woke up, grabbed a cuppa and sat in my kitchen while I logged on to Twitter. I needn't have worried about whether it would take off or not; by mid-morning the hashtag was the number one trending topic on Twitter and by the end of the day we had amassed an amazing 30 million impressions on social media.

It looked like a day dedicated to celebrating puns was a pretty popular thing. I'm not really the person to judge but perhaps more popular than other 'national' days, I wonder how much engagement days like 'National Town Planning Day', 'World Toilet Day' or 'World "Hello" Day' actually get? (If you would like to participate in 'World "Hello" Day' next year, apparently all you have to do is say 'hello' to ten people.)

On that first #UKPunday (8 February 2016) we also hosted a discussion, which was broadcast on BBC Radio, about puns and pun jokes. The panel of comedians and academics included the renowned sociologist, former president of the International Society for Humour Studies and author of many books on humour, Professor Christie Davies. Yep, there are now a few real-life academics who spend lots of time and energy considering the nature, form and value of pun-based comedy! The panel discussed what the key characteristics of puns are and why we groan when a pun is told. Puns are an especially British phenomenon but, as it turns out, aren't intrinsically British; we know this because of the uptick in traffic on Twitter each #UKPunDay when people in Australia wake up and start joining in. Our silly idea of a day celebrating puns has indeed gone global.

So, our first year was pretty popular and we thought we might be onto something. Something really silly but something that seemed to engage with loads of people. We decided to do it again and in our second year a similar number of folk got involved on Twitter but we also noticed a few companies and brands that were getting involved, including the Bank of England, Specsavers, National Trust, Currys PC World and many more have all joined in the silliness of #UKPunDay. Having been a fan all my life, I was especially delighted when the people behind *Coronation Street* tweeted some puns from the Corrie account. I'm not the best person to judge whether these corporate puns are any good, but we thought we would include some of them here to give you a flavour of what to expect next year …

In tonight's *Coronation Street*: David had his ID stolen! Now we just call him Dav …

CORONATION STREET

. . . .

We're going to see if we can get #CathedralPuns trending today. Chancel be a fine thing.

BRISTOL CATHEDRAL

. . . .

**Guys, we said our biscuits were too good
not to share ... not Cher!**

MCVITIE'S

. . . .

**'What's the first name of the guy who wrote
Robinson Crusoe and how sure are you?'**

'Daniel. Defo.'

ORKNEY LIBRARY

. . . .

What do you call a woman who can't draw? Tracy.

CORONATION STREET

. . . .

**What's Bruno Mars's favourite biscuit-related song?
Uptown Dunk.**

MCVITIE'S

. . . .

If you think they're rubbish, you know what to do next February. Get on Twitter, join in the pun, tweet your best puns and use #UKPunDay.

BIOGRAPHIES

Adele Cliff has had her work featured in Dave's 'Funniest Jokes of the Edinburgh Fringe' a record four years in a row. She has gigged internationally in Chicago, New York and the Adelaide Fringe, as well as writing for BBC Radio 4. She is the 2020 UK Pun Champion – the first woman to hold the title.

Richard Pulsford has been featured in Dave's Top 'Ten Jokes of the Edinburgh Fringe' (2019), the *Daily Mirror*'s 'Funniest Jokes of 2019' and was a finalist in The UK Pun Championships (2014–17; 2020). His comedy shows have had five full runs at Edinburgh Festival Fringe (2015–19). When not performing, Richard hosts the comedy-history podcast 'It Just So Happened'.

Richard Woolford is an award-winning idiot, absurdist, prop, pun, one-liner comedian and writer. He came second in The UK Pun Championships in 2019.

Philip Simon is an award-winning comedian (Jewish Comedian of the Year, 2015) who placed second in 2020's The UK Pun Championships. Since lockdown started, proving his viability, he's co-hosted the hugely successful podcast 'Jew Talkin' to Me?' and launched a children's joke show called 'School's Out Comedy Club'.

Kat Molinari is a comedian who began her career on the comedy circuit at the Frog & Bucket in Manchester, back in 2017. Since then, she has continued to perform around the north of England at venues including The Stand, XS Malarkey and is a regular at the all-female comedy night 'Laughing Cows'. She was a participant in 2020's The UK Pun Championships.

Chris Norton Walker is a one-liner comedian who has performed all over the world, including the UK, Europe and America. In 2020, Chris was a participant in The UK Pun Championships.

Colin Leggo (a.k.a. Colin 'The Punderdog' Leggo) is a Cornish, below-knee amputee, stand-up comedian who has been performing throughout the UK for the past 20 years. In 2019, he was named UK Pun Champion and went on to publish his own book, *Jokes for the Punderdog*.

Rob Thomas is the rubber-faced three-time finalist and 2018 winner of the UK Pun Championship. He is a full-time comedian and co-host of the popular weekly online show, *The UK Pun Off*.

Stevie Vegas (aka Steve the Juggler) is a professional comedy juggler and magician, born in Scotland, now living in England. He has been a finalist in The UK Pun Championships (2019 and 2020), three-time winner of UK Pun Off and a semi-finalist in Punderdome 3000. He writes new jokes every day on Twitter and is the author of two books on circus skills.

Joseph Murphy is a stand-up comedian known for his oddball performances. He was shortlisted for New Act of the Year in 2016 and was a finalist in The UK Pun Championships in 2019.

Andrew Tymms considers himself to be more punerable than most. He was a finalist in The UK Pun Championships in 2018 and has had his jokes published in the *Daily Mirror* and broadcast on BBC Radio 4 Extra's *Newsjack*. Following a nationwide search, Andrew was crowned Poundland's Gag Writer.

Iain MacDonald is a pun and one-liner comic from Glasgow who has been performing for the past 11 years. He is part of the online pun show *The UK Pun Off*, which broadcasts every Sunday and also hosts Buzzwords Comedy Bingo.

Lovdev Barpaga has been described by *Chortle* as the '21st Century Asian Ken Goodwin'. He was crowned UK Pun Champion in 2017, which you can't help noticing thanks to the amazing puns he's contributed to this book.

Masai Graham is a one-liner comedian from West Bromwich. In 2016, he came first in the Top 10 Edinburgh Jokes of the Fringe and was crowned UK Pun Champion.

Tony Cowards (a.k.a 'The Punasaurus') is an award-winning comedian and writer whose gags have shown up everywhere from TV and radio, to Christmas crackers and all other points in between. He has been described as 'the best joke writer around' by *GQ*.

Leo Kearse is a UK Pun Champion (2015) and has performed as 'Pun-Man', a superhero here to save humanity from observational comedy and long-form anecdote-based humour. He stopped doing puns because they're rubbish. He is now part of the raw, bold, American-inspired comedians taking the UK comedy circuit by storm. He was crowned Scottish Comedian of the Year (2017–18) and his 'Extinction Rebellion' video slamming woke lefties went viral.

Darren Walsh has been drawing cartoons and telling silly jokes since childhood. In 2014, he put those skills to good use by becoming UK Pun Champion.

Sean Hegarty is an Irish one-liner comedian who was a semi-finalist on *Ireland's Got Talent* and winner of 'Ireland's Funniest Joke'. His jokes, including a recent viral sensation concerning BBC's *Mastermind*, have totted up over 60 million views on social media. He is one of the top comedians working on the UK circuit today.

El Baldinho is a magician and prop comedian who you will find performing at festivals, comedy clubs and on TV in the UK and overseas. With a love for daft jokes, props and magic tricks, he really is the punjurer of the British comedy scene. In his spare time, he runs a magic shop where there's always a sale on – buy wand, get wand free.

Graham Musk has been entertaining audiences since 2014 with his puns and one-liners. He has a knack for seeing a twist in the joke and is a firm believer that words are his funny toy, which are there to be played with.

Laura Monmoth earned a 'Best New Show' nomination for her debut show at the 2018 Leicester Comedy Festival. Since then, she has travelled the country and stands in front of a screen making people laugh (occasionally) with an array of visual nonsense (constantly).

Kevin Hudson has been writing and performing comedy since attending a workshop in 2015. He is a regular at Leicester Comedy Festival, having performed two solo shows in 2019 and 2020. Kevin has reached the finals of the Silver Stand Up competition a record five times.

Paul Savage is a London-based, multiple award-winning comedian and cartoonist. He's the co-creator, co-writer and star of the cult hit gameshow, *Hell to Play*. His book of comics, *But Doctor, I am A Collection of Comics*, is now available. He lives on a narrowboat, which has been described as 'a mistake'.

Zahra Barri is a writer and stand-up comedian. Her debut novel, *Bird in the River*, was awarded runner-up in the Unpublished Comedy Novel category at the CWIP Book Prize in 2020.

Henry Dawe is an actor and writer based in Uppingham, Rutland. Since his play *Beyond the Pail* at Leicester Comedy Festival in 2016, he has continued to perform his work onstage in London and on the radio. *Play on Words* was released by TSL Publications in 2020, followed in 2021 by *Thirty Pieces of Pottiness*.

Sean Patrick is a New Acts of the Year Show (NATYS) finalist who performs at some of the top clubs in the UK. He is also the sophisticated half of the duo, Pat and Math.

Pauline Eyre has been performing comedy on and off – on till March 2020, then pretty much off since – for six years. Her first solo show, 'All Change', returns to a festival near you after this nightmare is over. Pauline is a 'confident and likeable performer' (*The Reviews Hub*) who has been applauded for her 'natural level of warmth and comic ability' (*Funny Women*).

Friz Frizzle is an award-winning comedian who has written jokes for chart-topping comedy albums, BBC Radio 4 and the West End.

Jenan Younis is the 2019 BBC New Voices Winner and has been a finalist in the Amused Moose New Act Competition, 99 Comedy Club Bursary, South East Comedian of the Year and runner-up in the 291 Club Contest. She is a regular contributor to the BBC Asian Network's Ladies Panel.

Nigel Lovell is a two-time finalist of The UK Pun Championships. His improvised, family-friendly, storytelling show, 'The Extraordinary Time-Travelling Adventures of Baron Munchausen', won the Leicester Comedy Festival Award for 'Best Kids' Show' in 2020. He hopes to see you, dear reader, at a comedy gig sometime soon.

Geoff Rowe is Director of Comedy for Union JACK Radio and co-founded Leicester Comedy Festival. He has interviewed countless comedians onstage – Sarah Millican, Alexei Sayle, Jasper Carrott, Romesh Ranganathan, Tom Allen, Jo Brand, Harry Hill – and has been on the judging panel for many competitions including the BBC New Comedy Awards, Funny Women, So You Think You're Funny and Edinburgh Comedy Award. He was interviewed on BBC Radio 4's *Front Row* as part of a special programme dedicated to Leicester Comedy Festival. He was awarded a British Empire Medal for his contributions to British comedy in 2013 and has received an Honorary Doctorate from De Montfort University.

Leicester Comedy Festival is the longest-running comedy festival in the UK and began as a final-year project organised by students studying at De Montfort University. The original programme of events included artists such as Rhona Cameron, John Shuttleworth, Matt Lucas, Harry Hill and Nick Park, while Sir Norman Wisdom and Tony Slattery were patrons of the festival in the first year. Since then, the festival has attracted 6,000 comedians and pulls in an audience of 135,000 each year over the nineteen-day comedy extravaganza that takes place in the heart of the city of Leicester. The festival has been featured in *The Times*, *Guardian*, *Metro*, *Telegraph* and on BBC Radio 2, BBC Radio 5 and *BBC News at Ten*.